CHOICES
AND
ILLUSIONS

Also by Eldon Taylor

Subliminal Learning

Subliminal Communication

Thinking Without Thinking

Subliminal Technology

Exclusively Fabricated Illusions

Just Be: A Little Cowboy Philosophy

Simple Things and Simple Thoughts

Little Black Book

Wellness: Just a State of Mind?

Plus hundreds of audio programs in English, Chinese, German, and Spanish

Website:
www.choicesandillusions.com

*** ***

Please visit Hay House USA: **www.hayhouse.com**®
Hay House Australia: **www.hayhouse.com.au**
Hay House UK: **www.hayhouse.co.uk**
Hay House South Africa: **orders@psdprom.co.za**
Hay House India: **www.hayhouseindia.co.in**

CHOICES AND ILLUSIONS

How Did I Get Where I Am,
and How Do I Get Where
I Want to Be?

Eldon Taylor

HAY HOUSE, INC.
Carlsbad, California
London • Sydney • Johannesburg
Vancouver • Hong Kong • New Delhi

Library of Congress Control Number: 2006940285

ISBN: 978-1-4019-1853-8

10 09 08 07   4 3 2 1
1st edition, June 2007

Printed in the United States of America

To the One Source, which created all
and with which we are intricately
interconnected—which includes you.

And to three special aspects of that One Source:

Roy, the wind beneath my wings;

Lois, who made sure the dream lived on;

and

Ravinder, who taught me the meaning of love.

Contents

Foreword

I lay back on the couch after finishing the book, and I closed my eyes.

At first I did not know why I had such a strong desire to read it again and to keep it on the nightstand close to me. Then I understood.

What every cell of my body was now experiencing was a new, powerful energy—revitalizing, rejuvenating, and inviting me to start taking action immediately. It was the energy that only hope can bring.

Yes, what this book brings to the reader is hope. It represents the life-saving ring thrown from an unexpected boat in the middle of the ocean to an exhausted swimmer who has lost his hope to reach the shore. It is the road back to the civilized world that an explorer, lost in an unfriendly jungle, suddenly discovers. It is the island with a landing field that a pilot of a plane almost out of fuel suddenly sees through the clouds above a rough ocean.

This book not only offers the reader a powerful insight into how the subconscious mind is dictating human behavior, but also offers the solution to regaining control of our existence on this planet.

And this is where the book stands out. We are finally able to acquire an understanding of not only why different things happen to us in our lifetime, but also how to start changing our destiny, no matter how far away we are from this knowing.

It is a book for all, the initiate as well as those still under the power of the illusions of this life.

It is a book designed to awaken the human consciousness.

What a wonderful relief to know that it is never too late to start changing, and also that we are always in full control of this process!

In my career as a neurologist, nothing produced a more dramatic effect on my patients' state of mind and their ability to recover from any condition than the sudden realization that they are themselves capable of influencing their own health, that they themselves are in the driver's seat, not the doctor.

After reading this book, the spiritualists will definitely claim Dr. Eldon Taylor as one of their own.

At the same time, the numerous scientific studies proving the validity of his approach in mind training with InnerTalk, done by reputable researchers, will place Dr. Taylor among scientists.

So, the only possible conclusion is that Dr. Taylor is both a scientist and a spiritualist.

By bridging these fields, he becomes a pioneer in what I believe could be considered the science of spirituality.

Last but definitely not least, Dr. Taylor is a humanitarian. Those who have become acquainted with his work over the years easily realize that his work is inspired by love, an unconditional love for a human race at crossroads and desperately needing to redefine itself in order to survive. His entire work and life are dedicated to this purpose.

I am firmly convinced that as long as people like Dr. Taylor exist, there is still hope for our planet to be saved and for our civilization to continue its progress toward enlightenment.

— **Cristian Enescu, M.D.**

*** ***

Preface

There is only one option when it comes to dedicating this work. This became very clear to me the other morning while acknowledging and giving thanks for all the blessings in my life. As I thought of many just from the day before, I remembered two small house martins playing with me while I watered the family's strawberry bed. One of the birds actually landed on my coffee cup in my left hand. The other bird sat less than six inches directly above my head on a branch of the elm tree that overhangs our strawberry bed. As if teasing me, they both then darted in and out of the stream of water from the garden hose held in my other hand. The entire scene was simply magical. The two birds apparently had no fear of me. I enjoyed their frolic and returned their teasing with an occasional movement of the stream of water, sometimes following them as they flew through, to land on a low-hanging branch.

For a few moments the birds and I knew no boundaries in terms of the traditional fear-laden relationship that all too often abides between man and nature. I even mused that it would have been something like this if the story of the Garden of Eden were to be drawn out in detail. There was a special sort of oneness—oneness from the One Source, the oneness that goes beyond the common denominator of atoms and molecules shared by all; it was the oneness of consciousness that abides in peace, balance, and harmony—harmony with all.

This vision in my mind of the events with two small birds and my feeling of happiness and joy that I believe was shared by the birds gives rise to the meaning behind the dedication to this book. To the realization of your birthright, may you find this work worthy of your time and energy.

Be well and happy.

*** ***

Introduction

"There has to be another way" is a popular motto in politics and in life. We get to this slogan when things simply don't work as well as we want them to. In our personal lives, we may discover that life is flying by and, like Little Black Sambo's tiger, we are just going in endless circles. Abraham Maslow believed that sooner or later mature people come to a point where the question becomes something like, "Is that all there is?" The principle labeled by Maslow as "self-actualization" then becomes important.

What is self-actualization? Like success, it can be many different things to different people. Like success, it is a level of satisfaction that arises from within ourselves: a sense of somehow making a difference to someone, a sense that our life has had purpose and meaning, that in some way or another, our life was worth living.

I have heard so-called motivational gurus suggest that success is all about money and power. I have heard them state such things as "Spirituality is something one does when one gets old." I do not believe that. For me, life is about a deeper meaning. Each of us has unique talents and abilities. My experience suggests that most fail to recognize their own birthright and find themselves trapped by beliefs that limit their personal possibilities. For me, life is about using those talents and abilities to the highest while serving an inner calling to make a difference with our lives.

It has been often stated that insanity is doing the same thing over and over while expecting a different outcome. To avoid this definition of insanity, sometimes it's necessary to convolute our models and reexamine our possibilities. This book is designed to assist and facilitate that alternative way of thinking for all who choose to read it.

I enjoy assembling puzzles. The most challenging puzzles require assembling small pieces into larger pieces before linking all the pieces in a complete picture. In a way, it is necessary to build the alternatives offered in this book in the same way. At times it may seem to you that the subject at hand is either a tangential path or a digression. I have therefore used my own story to weave together the many parts into a coherent whole.

*** ***

*The intuitive mind is a sacred gift
and the rational mind is a faithful servant.
We have created a society that honors
the servant and has forgotten the gift.*
— Albert Einstein

CHAPTER ONE

Choices and Illusions

Paraphrased, J. Krishnamurti said, "Choice is an illusion. Do I do this—do I do that—all of this is confusion. I can only choose when I'm confused. When I know clearly, there is no choice."[1] Thirty years ago, Benjamin Libet showed that there is activity in the subconscious within milliseconds before a conscious thought occurs. In other words, our so-called conscious thoughts are given us by our subconscious.[2]

People everywhere want to know how to improve their lives. Typically they believe that if they had more money, more power, more success, and better relationships, then they would be happy. Because of such beliefs, the world is full of fixers. There is a motivational guru on every corner, and there is no shortage of people waiting to spend their time and money on learning the "secrets to success." In a sense, I am no different; however, after more than thirty years of working with individuals in emotional distress, people seeking inner peace, athletes looking to win gold medals, sports organizations seeking to win championships, ordinary people trying to find a place in this world, and so on, I have learned this: *The model is all wrong!*

What Is Wrong?

What is wrong with more money or better relationships? Nothing! Then what do I mean that the model is wrong? The model is upside down, and it needs to be inverted—but before I can explain what I mean, it is necessary to digress a little first.

A Simple Digression

In the beginning there was a Big Bang. According to preeminent physicist Stephen W. Hawking, before the world of shoes and ships and sealing wax, there existed only singularity. Somehow singularity divided itself, and BANG—everything was born. Out of something we can only think of as super, super-compressed nothing—everything! To say this with a slightly different twist, from no thing came every thing. According to most major religions' creation stories, in the beginning the Source or Creator reflected upon itself (typically Himself) and divided Himself, creating everything. Notice that the words *singularity* and *Creator* are only reference points for a perspective. That is, if one is inclined to find a Grand Organizing Designer (G O D), then the chosen noun declares so; and if one tends toward avoiding such an agency, the noun again declares so. In other words, only one word separates these initial views of creation. Be that as it may, my point is more conspicuous. From the same source came everything. As such, everything is necessarily interrelated and interdependent. Later I will discuss this more fully. For now, I am asserting (and I am not the first to do so) that you, your neighbor, and the atoms in your pet are all participating in an interdependent state of being with the whole of the universe.

All right, let us use a little imagination and begin with the beginning. Please just assume for a moment that instead of being human, you are actually a chicken. Not just any chicken but a special, advanced species of chicken. Your species has a history of great thinkers. They have struggled with the first question, "Where did I come from?" Many philosophers have used your language to confuse everything: "Which came first, the chicken or the egg?" Your science-minded best have insisted that the question was irrelevant, stating flatly that you originated from the evolution of a single cell built from molecular building blocks, ever adapting to the conditions of your physical environment, despite the fact that the very building materials needed to construct the first DNA molecule did not exist—and only DNA can create DNA.[3] Many of your psychologists have advanced the general opinion that your basic need for survival, your drive mechanisms—fight, flight, feeding, and breeding—underlie most behavior. Indeed, survival-of-the-fittest mechanisms, basic drives necessary for the propagation of your species, explain advanced theories defining behavior in ways even psychologists disagree over. Some of your metaphysical teachers are preaching a theory of imperfection and an earth age of just a few thousand years, despite overwhelming evidence to the contrary. According to this theory, chickens could have been created perfectly, but they were not. They were made to suffer, and the more they suffered and the better they suffered, the more likely they were to be saved, or go to chicken heaven. Chicken believers in this paradigm worked to convert other chickens to their belief, and believe it or not, many chickens converted. Life sucks and then you die, but when you die, something wonderful happens if you have demonstrated your willingness to be punished for your imperfect deficient self—the self the Creator created.

Your social scientists have quantified group behavior and provided statistical inferences as a result. They are now able to make many predictions about the nature of your social organization, mating habits, and more. Specialized groups have even developed interdisciplinary theories, including those that have mapped your mind and informed you what every corner of it was up to, how it processed information, and so on. Your sciences are truly amazing. Why, even the DNA of your species has been mapped. Such an advanced species you are!

With all this advancement, there are still group chicken houses with individual nests that make up your chicken yard or community. Now let's add just a little extra imagination and use a story to get the full picture of what I'm trying to describe. We'll just imagine a creature raised by the chickens in this story.

It seems a female eagle fell from her nest at a very young age. She wandered until she happened onto a chicken yard, where an older hen adopted and raised her. The chickens taught the eagle the way of chickens. She learned to dig holes and wiggle down into them on hot days to stay cool. She learned to scratch with her talons and soon became valued for her ability to scratch deep into the earth. She learned many things from the chickens, and despite her size was loved by many. She was secure in her chicken house surrounded by her friends and adopted mother. Still, she sometimes felt out of place, uneasy in ways she could not explain, unfulfilled and unnatural. Her friends would reassure her. They would say things like "Other chickens don't always lay an abundance of eggs" and "Some hens make only a little noise when they do lay an egg." She would confide in her closest friends, and most would reassure her that this was life and she would adjust in time. She needed only to try harder; after all, her biological mother had failed her. This was comforting, for it wasn't her fault—her mother was to blame. Unlike Jonathan Livingston Seagull,[4] there was no great Seagull to teach her otherwise. So, her potential, the possibilities in life, went altogether unknown until one day a male eagle flying overhead spotted her grubbing in the chicken yard.

She is such a grand eagle, he thought, as he descended to speak with her, but one of the chickens caught a glimpse of his shadow and called to the others. The female eagle, who was called Nina, quickly scurried with the chickens to the chicken house, where they hid the rest of the afternoon. The male eagle was confused but determined.

Days passed before he gained another opportunity. Darting out of the sky with the sun on his face so as not to cast a shadow, he cut off Nina's retreat almost before any in the yard were aware he was approaching. The chickens hid in the chicken house—not one dared to venture out even to see what might be happening to Nina.

Trapped by the male eagle, Nina crouched down in fear, almost paralyzed by her expectation.

"Why are you here?" he asked.

Unable to answer, Nina could only tremble and look down.

"What are you doing here?" he went on. "I have never seen an eagle nesting with chickens, though I've heard such things happen. Have you lost your mind, girl?"

Nina looked up. She suddenly had an idea, for she was a smart chicken. "Did you call me an eagle?" she meekly inquired.

"Of course! You are one. Have you not looked at yourself? Have you not felt the urge to stretch your wings and soar? Have you not felt out of place with these chickens? Do you think those talons were made to dig in the earth? I have watched you for days now. You do everything the chickens do. Why?"

Nina stared in his eyes. They were large and brown. His pupils were dark black and nearly filled his entire eye. He looked as though he could see forever. "You've watched me?" she asked.

"Yes, I've watched you, but I don't understand. You are capable of so much. I could tell you stories for days of adventures and sights that have filled my life—and that should fill yours. You were created with such unlimited potential—you simply don't belong in this yard. You are a beautiful and capable eagle. Can't you see that?"

Nina felt stronger now. Something was wrong with this eagle. *He must have some Messianic complex,* she thought. Imagine his telling her she could soar. Nina said, "So I'm an eagle and I can soar and do things you can show me that I have never done? Is that right?"

"It's in you, girl. Follow your feelings. Be natural. You're not a chicken, I promise."

"So then," Nina continued, "since I'm an eagle, you're not going to hurt me."

"Of course not—what nonsense is that?"

"Well, then," Nina confidently added, "show me. Step aside so I could leave if I choose to."

With that, the male eagle stepped out of Nina's path. She seized the opportunity and made the best of her plan, running straight for the chicken house. Once inside she told the chickens how she had outsmarted that dumb old eagle. They all laughed and rewarded her with their chicken appreciation, "You're such a good smart chicken, Nina!" The old rooster even spoke nicely to her. "I'm proud of you, Nina—you certainly did outsmart that eagle."

By now, the moral to this story is obvious. Most people have been enculturated to accept and believe certain things that may, and likely do, betray their real potential. Like the chickens in the chicken yard, we have all been *imprinted*. Behavioral scientists use this term for the process whereby animals seek to be accepted by imitating their peers. An eagle or a duckling raised in a chicken yard will behave like a chicken, and so forth. The first tutorial this story provides gives rise to this question:

How many chicken beliefs limit you and alienate you from your potential now?

Robert Laing wrote more than thirty years ago in his book *The Politics of Experience:* "The condition of self-alienation is the condition of the normal man." Alan Watts, in his book *Psychotherapy East and West,* quoted from a speech Carl Jung gave to a group of ministers in 1938: "That I feed the beggar, that I forgive an insult, that I love my enemy—all of these are undoubtedly great virtues. What I do unto the least of my brethren, that I do unto Christ. But what if I should discover that the least amongst them all, the poorest of all beggars, the most impudent of all offenders, yea, the very fiend himself—that these are within me, and that I myself stand in need of the alms of my own kindness, that I myself am the enemy that must be loved—what then?"

Let us imagine the human condition programmed with negative expectations. Like fleas in a flea circus, we have been raised to believe that some invisible dome defines who we are, how high we can soar, our basic parameters of life expectancy and health, and so forth—self-imposed limitations that we are totally unaware of, boundaries that we honor despite their unreality and the truth that our sages, geniuses, entrepreneurs, and heroes have all told us to ignore them. But, like our female eagle, we believe we know better or we simply do not know how to pierce those limitations.

Take a look at the nine stars on the following page. Using a pencil or pen, connect the centers of all nine stars with four straight lines without lifting your instrument from the page. Try it, if not with an instrument, then in your mind.

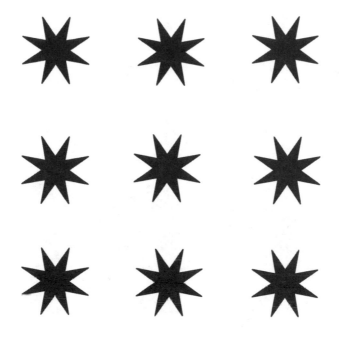

Now turn the page and see how easy it is to connect them with four lines if you do not accept the implied boundary of the stars.

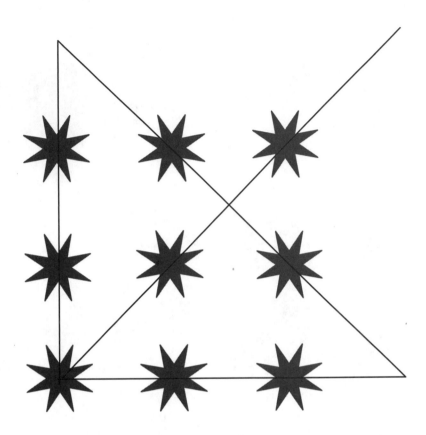

If you are like almost everyone else, extending the lines beyond the so-called boundary of the stars is not something that occurred to you. If it does not come to mind, it is not among your possible choices. Let us illustrate that concept further with a story, because stories stick with us, as do pictures, and are often worth much more than the words that it takes to tell them.

Imagine that you're visiting New York City for the first time. You're amazed at the skyline—all those immensely tall buildings. You visit a beautiful area of high-rise condominiums. These are truly luxurious condos, all with balconies suspended above the sidewalk. It's a glorious day. The sun is out, and the slight breeze you feel is warm and comforting. The air is unusually fresh for any part of the world, and you're simply walking, taking in the sights and sounds, and enjoying the day to the fullest. It's New York, and you have heard stories about this city, but it's light and bright and pleasant, and you walk on, thinking of all that you'll tell your friends back home.

Suddenly, from the third-floor balcony above you, a flowerpot falls and slams onto your head. The pot is deflected onto the sidewalk and shatters. You're not seriously hurt, but your head is hurting. You feel a bulge rapidly building into a rather large knot. Your scalp has a nasty abrasion that burns when you touch it, and on your hand is a small amount of blood. The suddenness and pain have raised your adrenaline level. That old fight/flight mechanism has kicked in, and the neurochemicals are flowing. Anger begins to rise. Now you have some choices.

What would you do?

Let's think about that and explore some possibilities—possibilities given me over many years of lecturing. You could go up to that third-floor condo and shove you know what where. You might get there only to discover that the owner is a defensive linebacker for some professional football team and his biceps are larger than your waist. Then you might change your plan.

What else could you do? Some might think of this as an opportunity. "I'll sue this fat cat. Anyone who puts a flowerpot too close to the edge of the balcony railing, just waiting to fall on someone, should be educated. What if it had fallen on a small child or a baby in a buggy passing under the balcony? Suing will be a quickie—they'll settle out of court. That'll teach them to be more careful in the future. Concussion and whiplash—I wonder what those are worth."

What else could you do? Well, some might think the incident was a sign from the gods. It's time to be metaphysical—after all, the blow might have delivered enlightenment. It might even be like one of those lightning strikes in which the person struck gains special metaphysical or parapsychological abilities. Like John Travolta in the movie *Phenomenon,* such a person can do or solve almost anything. It's like instantly acquiring the knowledge of the universe.

What else could you do?

William James is credited with coining the term *pragmatic*. What is pragmatic? In our instance, it is simply responding to the stimuli in a manner that works for you. What would work for you? What if you picked up the flower off the hot sidewalk and took it to a florist for repotting? What if you selected a very nice pot, had the plant repotted, and then returned it to the owner with an explanation of why it was in a new pot? You could say something like this: "Your flower pot fell from your balcony and hit me on the head. The pot smashed against the sidewalk, so I took the beautiful flower to the florist and had it repotted for you. Here it is. I hope you like the new pot."

Of all the things you might do, what do you think would make you feel the best? Of all the things you might do, what do you think would change those neurochemicals from fight/flight to growth and pleasure?

An acquaintance of mine, Dr. Bruce Lipton, models the body this way. It, like a government, has two budgets: One budget is for defense, and the other is for growth. As such, when the body goes to defense (fight/flight), it cannot grow. When the body is at peace, the budget turns entirely toward growth (optimal health and wellness). If you think of this budget for a moment (we will return to this issue later) and realize that in modern man fight and flight have been replaced with anxiety and depression, it's easy to see that this heightened state of arousal is normal, albeit unhealthy. That is, anxiety and depression are states of alarm (fight/flight), and most people have plenty of stimuli in their everyday lives to keep the body aroused.

So, of the choices with respect to our flowerpot story, which choice would serve you best? The answer is obvious. But since it is so obvious, why wasn't it recognized right away? Here is my point. In a scenario such as our flower-pot story—and believe me we all have similar scenarios, like the person who cuts us off in traffic or pushes into line in front of those already lined up—why do we fail to see the obvious and instead choose the lesser?

**When the obvious should be so clear, why is it
that so many of us fail even to
recognize the alternative?**

Choice? Do I do this or do I do that? What choice do I have if I cannot see an alternative to the lesser of evils? What, then, does one mean when one believes in free will and choice and yet ducks responsibility? As with freedom and democracy, responsibility accompanies choice. Whether with free will or freedom of speech, each of us has a responsibility to become informed and behave intelligently as a result. Then how does one escape the narrow, self-imposed boundaries that predispose our so-called choices?

Before undertaking an answer for that last question, it will be useful to understand a little more about the human condition—how we learn our self-limiting notions and what and how we perceive what we perceive.

*** ***

Flatter me, and I may not believe you.
Criticize me, and I may not like you.
Ignore me, and I may not forgive you.
Encourage me, and I may not forget you.
— William Arthur

CHAPTER TWO

Creating Self

Most of us have been enculturated during maturation to accept and believe certain things that may, and likely do, limit our real potential. Like chickens in the chicken yard, we have all been imprinted. Behavioral scientists use this term to refer to the process whereby animals seek to be accepted by imitating their peers. For example, a duckling raised in a chicken yard will behave like a chicken, and so forth. How many chicken beliefs limit you now?

**Most of us have been enculturated during maturation
to accept and believe certain things that may,
and likely do, limit our real potential.**

Estimations by many suggest that for every unit (bit) of positive, affirming information one processes, 90 bits or more of negative information is received. In other words, for every time one is praised or reassured, 90 times they are fed the opposite information. As a result, most find themselves trapped in self-limiting beliefs about their abilities, their intelligence, their worth—even their health and happiness. One study showed that belief predicated not only vocation but also the cause of death. That study, conducted by Dr. David Phillips at the University of California–San Diego, evaluated the Asian belief in birth signs. In Asia, one born under a sign, such as the Dog, knows what one is good at and therefore probably what one will do vocationally. The sign also informs the cause of death—say, cardiac disease. The research showed clearly a positive correlation between belief and events, no matter the lifestyle of the individual. In other words, clean living and self-denial did not keep away cancer if the birth sign suggested that as the cause of death.[5]

In the spring of 1991, I conducted a survey among physicians who had consented to permit their patients to use a special experimental subliminal InnerTalk program that I had created for cancer remission. (I will cover this technology in depth later.) The aim of the study was to look at life expectancy in comparison with the actual mortality rates of cancer patients who used the subliminal program. The questionnaire went to physicians whose patients had received the subliminal program two to four years earlier. The twelve questions were on a scale of 1 to 5:

1. Strongly disagree
2. Disagree
3. Neutral
4. Agree
5. Strongly agree

The twelve questions consisted of four general categories:

1. The patient's attitude toward the disease before the patient used the program.
2. The patient's attitude toward the disease after the patient used the program.
3. The patient's survival and quality of life.
4. How the physician felt about his/her patients believing their health could be affected by the patient's mind.

This survey yielded many interesting findings, including significant remission rates, for 38 percent of the so-called terminal patients were in remission at the conclusion of the study. Another overwhelming result might surprise you. Of the four categories, which do you think would be the most consistent factor affecting the life expectancy, or remission rate, in the patient?

Most people believe that it is the patient's attitude, even though those same people would say that a terminal disease such as cancer could not be affected just by changing the patient's attitude. It wasn't the patient's attitude, however, but the physician's attitude that was the most important factor in determining whether the patient lived or died.

The physician's attitude was the most important factor in determining whether the patient lived or died.

If the physician did not believe that the patient's involvement with the subliminal tape or the patient's attitude could affect the cancer, the patient died, regardless of which treatment procedure was used—radiation, chemotherapy, and so on. The patient died regardless of the patient's own attitude toward the disease or its ultimate outcome. The one factor present in virtually every case was the physician's attitude.

Taking into account only those patients whose physicians agreed, to some degree, that the mind played a role in the patient's health, then the survival/remission rate increased to 46 percent. If we look at those physicians who strongly agreed that the mind or attitude of the patient is important to health and/or health care, the survival/remission rate increased to 60 percent. Narrowing the field still further, where both the patient and the physician tended to believe strongly that the mind played a role in wellness, the rate of survival/remission increased to 100 percent.

To me, this study showed clearly that not only is the mind capable of healing the body but what individuals "believed they were capable of" directly influenced the outcome. This power of "self-belief" was also demonstrated in a landmark research project by Dr. Ellen Langer that reversed certain characteristics of aging.

Dr. Langer of Harvard University took "old people" into the country-side where they were isolated for one week. The older persons were exposed to "photographs, newspapers, radio (music and advertising) and discussions that were strictly limited to topics current twenty years earlier. At the end of the week, the group became younger looking by three years, gained weight, behaved more independently, and could actually hear better." When the "old people" stopped believing they were old and were reimmersed in a younger time frame, then aging was reversed.[6]

Another revealing study that speaks directly to the power of self-belief is one carried out by Dr. Martin Seligman. In this study, dogs were placed on an electric grid. To begin with, the dog could get up and move to a part of the floor without a grid in order to avoid electric shock. However, after the grid was expanded to include the entire floor—when there was no escape from the grid—dogs just gave up. They lay helpless and whimpered, regardless of whether or not an electric shock was applied. Their immune and encodocrine systems almost shut down. There seemed to be no hope, so they seemingly gave up wanting to live. In the giving-up belief, I suppose there was no reason to live, no escape, and their mindset communicated to the body, and the body responded accordingly.[7]

Every day the media inundates its audience with messages of disease. These messages typically seek to sell some cure or antidote—but to sell the cure, they must first announce or sell the disease. These so-called commercials create belief and expectation. When you tell someone, "Don't touch wet paint," the person usually touches it. When the media tells you day after day what will sicken and even kill you, how much death and disease are they creating? I believe that it is actually criminal, or it should be, that dis-ease is sold this way. (I cover this subject in detail in my book *Wellness: Just a State of Mind?*)

The media also provides images of success, ways to dress, beauty, and so on. These images sell such goods as sports cars, cosmetics, and the like—good for the economy, maybe, but if the image is not exactly as one sees oneself, then the image suggests a lack on the part of the viewer. Movies such as *First Blood* romanticize getting even. Heroes and heroines build images of courage and strength through violent acts against "bad guys." Children copy this. Promoters sell it not just through the movies but also through such add-ons as toys. What child has seen *Star Wars* and not also wanted a laser sword like those of the Jedi masters?

Peers, parents, teachers, and others tend to be insensitive. Their words, looks, gestures, and even jokes often make people feel inferior. We all long to be included, wanted, important. So, all in all, the negative so far outweighs the positive that it is no wonder so many people feel as though their real self is trapped in some empty shell while life speeds by. It is easy to become so accustomed to this state of affairs that we celebrate it with bumper stickers and sayings, such as "TGIF" and "I don't get even—I get evener!"

Compensation is a psychological mechanism identified first by H. S. Sullivan. When individuals lack confidence and esteem, they often compensate by extracting their worth from another. An unconscious nonsense belief seems to propel them into behavior that ridicules, offends, and hurts others. Physical violence is just another way of acting out pain or fear—not that it is really any different in an emotional sense. The abuses they dish out can be thought of as their own inner insecurities being compensated for by making someone else feel insecure—as they do. It's all a rapid downward spiral that leads to anything but true happiness and success.

Like Nina, the female eagle, it is easy to outsmart those who may offer an alternative to the known—the comfortable. Small minds condemn what they do not understand. Like Nina, most people do not accept that within themselves is a power that can change all of those self-limiting, self-destructive beliefs, a power that can indeed result in manifesting a person so self-responsible that he/she walks and lives above the fray—in the world but not of the world. This is truly your birthright. Life is not designed to be only struggle.

Mark Twain tells a story in his work *Letters to Earth*. In the story, the archangels are deciding where to hide God. It is suggested that they hide him on the moon or deep beneath the surface of the sea, and so forth. However, each suggestion eventually leads the archangels to conclude that mankind is too smart for that—sooner or later they would find God. So where do they decide to hide Him? Within every human being—for "the last place mankind will look is within," they conclude.

Within every human being exists a propensity for greatness. The gifts may vary, and the greatness may live out in a vast array of alternatives—say, from carpentry to rocket ships—but the gift that gives one true self-respect, lifts the spirit from "same old, same old," resides within. These are not just words or some lofty notion, as will be shown in later chapters. This potential resides within each one of us—but if so, then why is it so often denied?

Every individual essentially has a self-representation that is rehearsed and eventually actualized. The process begins by fantasizing at a very early age. We fantasize a script, perhaps one of those from some Hollywood production. We begin rehearsing it, and we either abandon it to take up a new one or practice it until we role-play that script as who we are. Practicing the script sooner or later automates the behavior. Our imprinting environment plays a significant role in the alternative scripts available to us. If the parents are uncaring and abusive, so are the children, and so forth. If warmth and friendliness lead to embarrassment, then cold and aloof compensate. If honesty gets us into trouble, then deception becomes a defense strategy, and so forth.

It is much more complicated than expressed here, but simply, it is also just this way. In fact, every one of us divides ourselves among four essential views of ourselves. These four faces include the following:

1. Our actual self
2. Our ideal self
3. Our ought-to-be self
4. Our desired self

These categories were originally developed by P. A. D. Singer to show how the different selves conflict with each other.[8] I will use it differently.

Most of us are aware of a so-called actual self. This is the self that has failed in ways we often will not share with others. This is the private self. This self holds the thoughts we wish we did not have, the acts we wish we had not done, our beliefs about our worth, our attractiveness, and so forth. It is the self of our secrets and our ambitions. It is the self that most try to change in some way or another at some time in their life—perhaps even perpetually.

The actual self pales by comparison to our ideal self. The ideal self is often a construct built by our culture. This self would live a perfect life—without error and therefore without room for growth.

Then there is our "ought-to-be self." This is the self full of all our learned "shoulds" and "oughts." This self differs from our ideal self in the sense that many of the oughts are not ours—they are the oughts of our culture, our society—but deep down inside they are not ours. Sometimes these oughts are the result of rules that make little or no sense to us; sometimes the oughts are of codependent negotiations such as those implied when Mom said things like, "If you loved me, you would not behave that way," or "If you loved me, you would do what I said," and so forth. Still, even when one recognizes the source and the nature of the ought relationship from which the oughts themselves arise, they often persist.

Finally, there is the desired self. Somewhere among all of our other selves is a self that we believe we could be. This is the self we long for, especially when we are young and planning our future. It is also the source of much discontent in our later life if the desires have not been fulfilled—and they rarely, if ever, are.

The ought-to-be self, desired self, and ideal self share certain commonalities, but they also differ remarkably. There is psychic tension among them and in their totality, substantial tension between them and our so-called actual self.

Now, there's one more thing I wish to add before continuing. The actual self is seldom the true actual self. The actual self is the self of self-perception and therefore is complete with every believed limitation that accompanies one's private self-perception.

If we think back to Nina in the chicken yard, some additional clarity can be added that translates directly to most human eagle/ chickens. Within each of us is an almost unlimited possibility—the eagle potential. Within each of us is the sum of all those conflicts, failures, negative message units, and the like—the so-called sum of self-imposed, albeit typically culturally imposed, limitations. Within each of us exists the need to be accepted and the fear of loss—loss of friends, respect, acceptance, love, and so forth. Within all of us is a cry to soar, in the vernacular of the eagle, and at the same time, a fear of leaving the comfort of our little chicken houses. Within all of us are the secret failures, low or base desires, deeds, and so forth that constitute our perceived actual selves. All of this tension typically holds us almost rigid and stiff, nearly cataleptic, if the change truly threatens any of our four self-images. Now, to add fuel to the fire, change is what most of us truly desire. A true Catch-22—damned if we do and damned if we don't.

So how do we safely discover, or uncover, our true potential. What are the limits to our potential—or how high is up?

Innumerable biographies of great people share at least one common denominator—they believed they could do something everyone else, or at least nearly everyone, thought was impossible. These people are the heroes of our world. What made them so convinced they could succeed, despite the crowds that argued to the contrary? That's the next question. For if every one of us possessed that conviction and power, would we not all succeed? If the solution was so obvious as to negate choice—that is, if we saw so clearly our direction, ambition, goal, purpose, and so forth, that there was nothing to choose between—what could stop us from realizing that path?

Let us now look a little deeper into the nature of mind and perception, particularly perceptual defense mechanisms—indeed, defense mechanisms in general.

*** ***

*The only way to discover the limits of the possible
is to go beyond them into the impossible.*
— Arthur C. Clark

CHAPTER THREE

What We Perceive and Fail to Perceive

If choice is an illusion, what other illusions might we live with? This is such a large subject that we won't even try to take on that question in a comprehensive way. We will, however, look at it sufficiently here to clarify for our purposes the most relevant illusions.

Our first illusion is due to language. Language labels everything, and once that is done, that which is labeled is "diminished," in the words of Kierkegaard.[9] Nouns are the names of persons, places, and things, yet many nouns refer to things that do not exist. For example, take the noun *griffin*. Arguably, a mythical creature matches this word, but no such creature actually exists. Further, some nouns are really about form, not things. Take the word *chair*. In the Platonic sense, *chair* refers to a form, that of "chairness." When we attempt to describe a chair we can be surprised at the definitional ambiguities. Not all chairs have arms or four legs, are stationary, or even are meant to be sat upon, yet somehow when we see a chair, we recognize it as a chair.

Our first illusion is due to language.

Years ago I wrote a piece titled "Sticks and Stones Will Break My Bones but Words Will Slice and Dice Me." The article bared a penetrating conclusion: words do more damage to most people in our culture than things do. It is not the word itself or even Webster's definition that is damaging or fearsome; rather, it is the emotive value attached to the words.

It is easy to note the fear of many when they hear words of rejection, words that make fun or are excessively and inappropriately critical, words that condemn, words that negatively label, such as *ugly, stupid, loser, failure,* and so forth. Words, however, have still other emotional domains that they anchor or that are like search words in a web browser. When input, they trigger a host of related sites stored deep in our memory. Indeed, due largely to our educational system and culture, most words can be said to have values. Think about it. Even so-called innocuous descriptors such as color have value attached. Some colors are preferred over others, some colors are simply obnoxious, and for some, an emotional disturbance or trauma can be connected to a color.

Our thinking system is such that we all have been taught relative values and judgments. They are reflected in our description of everything we know about ourselves and the world around us. For most, at least in our culture, words are generally thought to be capable of accurately describing at least the world around us, including ourselves, our feelings, our thoughts, and of course, our reasons.

Our world is so dependent upon words, semantics, that it is hard to imagine thinking without them. Indeed, thinking seems to presuppose semantic possibilities; after all, how else would we be able to communicate or understand our thinking? Even the images in our dreams are thought to be better understood when we can explain them. So dominant is this thinking priority, this semantic communication necessity, that a failure to be able to communicate linguistically an idea, a feeling, an urge, an intuition, an image, a sense, etc., is thought to be the result of either inadequate education or inadequate basic genetic equipment. After all, where would we be if we couldn't ask such meaningful questions as *What did that mean to you? How did that make you feel? What do you mean by that? Describe the sense or feeling or image or how do you know it is a valid intuition and not just fanciful thinking?*

Not only is our world known through semantics—linguistic communication with self and others—but it is modeled by each of us in just this same way. To say that knowing the world through words is quite different from knowing the world through actual sensing participation is just obvious and trite. To say knowing oneself—or better still, modeling oneself and one's behavior through this same word lens—should be even more conspicuously ridiculous. Still, for most, it is precisely through the lens of words that both self and the world are known.

We know much more than we know, at least about ourselves. We all came into this world knowing how to naturally sense our environment, how to explore and provide honest feedback about our feelings, how to allow our imaginations to deliver intuitions and images without challenge, and then to feel them for that value alone. But alas, we all learned to be educated and to cherish thinking, not just free thinking, but thinking according to the taught order of correct thinking (e.g., mathematics, logic, etc.). Once the rules of thinking were learned, we were graded on our ability to reproduce the method in our every walk and talk of life, including how we talk to ourselves.

One day, incorporating our learned methods of thinking with our acquired meanings or values to events and words, we subverted our natural selves to the higher order of being what we should be—unnatural. Our extended dependent maturation made us particularly vulnerable to such basic needs as protection and nourishment and therefore, additionally vulnerable to supplanting ourselves with the personification of what was expected, what was accepted, what was tolerated, what brought reward, and what avoided punishment. To that extent, even in rebellion, we formed a bond with a self that was perhaps alien to our true selves. Moreover, we anchored all of this emotional memory in and with words, and then we explained ourselves using a socially acceptable vocabulary such as, "It's okay to get even." This only further masked our real feelings (insecurities such as fear and isolation) while encouraging additional distortions. Of course, there was always the alternative—outright rejection— although this too is a distorted perspective. For many this distortion translates into a poor self-image: "I'm no good." My research with incarcerated criminals suggests there is yet another step, or level, to this kind of distortion, the step from high self-alienation to and including high social alienation. When this occurs, the self-image is verbalized more like this: "I'm no good, and neither are you. You (people like you) did it to me. You (someone) made me this way."

As semantic descriptions are built, semantic reactions or responses are encoded and a semantic belief system is coherently hinged to the degree that coherence is possible within the rules of thinking as we have learned them. When incoherence is obvious, a defense mechanism is employed to mask the failure, and semantic distortions are created. To a cognitive psychologist, this kind of thinking is known as cognitive dissonance, or holding two opposing views/opinions/beliefs without recognizing that they are mutually exclusive. A good practical example of that is the belief that money is the source of all evil and the belief that money will improve the quality of life. The outside world, together with the inside world, has at this point become more or less a series of semantic anchors composed of semantic descriptions, semantic reactions, and semantic beliefs and distortions all seamed together like a fisherman's net with semantic references definitionally reinforcing each other.

Our world, to use the words of Alfred Korzybski, has now become, perhaps more often than any sane person would like to admit, false to fact and therefore necessarily distorted. As Korzybski puts it, the difference between sanity and insanity can be found in false-to-fact distortions that are semantic in nature.[10] It is precisely the mechanism of semantic distortions that underlies thinking processes that are or become neurotic or psychotic. It is also this same mechanism that gives rise to self-sabotaging behavior and self-limiting beliefs. This very same mechanism—and *mechanism* is a good word because the process becomes so automatic that it operates without conscious awareness—martials our defenses to action whenever our semantic descriptions, semantic reactions, and semantic beliefs and distortions (semantic processes) are challenged. In fact, the unconscious pervasiveness of the mechanistic nature of these semantic processes is such that even the most knowledgeable of specialists on the matter must maintain a constant vigil to guard against them. This may explain why an individual can be very successful in a given field and fail miserably in another.

Our language usage, the value and meaning we attach to words, can blind rational thinking. We could effectively argue that genius escapes this language barrier, for genius goes beyond the boundaries, sees the common differently, gains a perspective not formerly found. Our world not only assigns values to words but also insists on a sort of "is-ness" property that somehow gives the word an existence of its own. The label, the noun, becomes the thing. The verb may even vicariously become the action.

We all can be fooled by word propositions that address definitional meanings, is-ness, and rules, the so-called logic of our methods and use (or misuse) of language and thinking. A theist could argue that God is all-powerful, while the atheist might refute this claim with such a question as, "Can God create a stone so large He can't lift it?" Word traps and their confusion have led to many atrocities.

It's easy to forget the nature of personal truth when it masquerades in an argument of reason. Logic and linguistics make assertions about many things that are simply false to facts. For example, logic asserts that a gallon is equal to a gallon. This is simply not true from many perspectives, including the most obvious. A gallon of water added to a gallon of alcohol does not equal two gallons of combined fluid. Ergo, $1 + 1 = 2$ is not necessarily so in the "real" world. No two things are alike in every way. Additionally, it is not possible to know the so-called total of anything. Words are not the things they represent, and what they are supposed to represent is much more, and much less, than could ever be written. Indeed, as has been said many times, probably in its most noteworthy form by the philosopher Ludwig Wittgenstein, "whatever we say about something, it is also not that." Words are not things, and word things, such as a *griffin*, do not necessarily exist.

So if our words trick us, then that "stream of consciousness," in the words of William James, also tricks us. All those inner conversations with ourselves, all the self-talk, trick us just as assuredly. Still, that is not the only illusion our minds are capable of.

If our words trick us, then that "stream of consciousness," in the words of William James, also tricks us.

For example, there are many visual illusions. We often see what is not there and often fail to see what is. Further, we are very suggestible and can easily see what is suggested. Let's take some common illusions for purposes of illustration and turn this idea into experience. The following illusion is commonly circulated on the Internet.

Stare a moment at the picture above and you will find that the gears seem to move. Change your gaze from center to corners, and different gears seem to move or move more rapidly. Of course, nothing moves at all.

Art by Antonio Zamora
Derived from a design by A. Kitaoka
Reprinted with permission

(For links to this and many other illusions that work better in color on a computer screen, go to **www.choicesandillusions.com**)

The next picture should be looked at in a special way. It appears on a page by itself for this reason. When you turn the page, look only at the page. Stare at the center three dots. Concentrate on those dots for one minute. Stare only at the dots, and after that minute, turn and look at a blank wall. Just gaze at the wall for approximately 45 seconds. Allow yourself to look rather unfocused, but keep your gaze at the same space on the wall. Keep looking at the blank wall, even if you think nothing is going to happen. Something unique will happen, and you should know that this can be done with any number of pictures. What you will see will amaze you, even startle you.

Turn the page and follow these instructions. Enjoy!

Okay, you just saw a dove soar upwards. The illusion on the next page was chosen to demonstrate how emotions can be tangled with illusions. Everyone knows that a thirsty person in the desert can see a mirage (the illusion of an oasis or simply water) and lose rational abilities in favor of desperate emotions. The next illusion is an emotion-laden illusion. It will evoke a strong emotional response in accordance with a line of personal belief system. The illusion may please, it may inspire, it may anger—but the point of the illusion in this context becomes very clear: a simple illusion can evoke strong emotional reactions.

Once again, follow the instructions. Stare this time at the center four dots. Concentrate on those dots for one minute. Stare only at the dots, and after that minute, turn and look at a blank wall. Just gaze at the wall for approximately 45 seconds. Allow yourself to look rather unfocused, but keep your gaze at the same space on the wall. Keep looking at the blank wall, even if you think nothing is going to happen

Turn the page and follow these instructions.

(Please note: these kinds of illusions can be found anywhere and are widely circulated on the Internet.)

The next picture illustrates both our abilities to see and not to see, or to see differently. This is the rather famous witch and maiden illusion. At first glance, you will see either a witch or a beautiful young maiden. You are typically unable to see both at the same time—at least with conscious recognition per se. Shift the focus slightly, and the image changes. That is, if you see the witch first, shift focus and you will see the maiden.

Here is another either/or image that is quite famous. It is known as "faces and vases." See if you can see both.

The next illusion involves dots. It reminds me of the hidden faces one used to find in the Sunday newspaper. Finding and counting the faces to win something was the purpose of the ad.

Below is a scattering of inkblots. Take a look and see what you see.

If you look closely, you will see a dalmatian with its nose down, sniffing the ground. You can make out the dog's ear, snout, shoulder, and left leg first, and the rest fills itself in. Once you see the dog clearly, you cannot help but see it—like the hidden faces in the old Sunday newspapers.

The image below is also a common illusion. Our visual reference system often distorts images according to the background. The circle in the center is really a perfect circle.

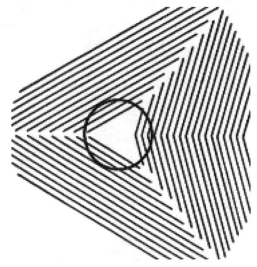

One of my favorite illusions cannot be done on paper. All of us know that we have a blind spot, an area that we do not see—our brains make it up. I encourage you to try this illusion. On my website is a spinning disk (**www.innertalk.com/hypnodisk/hypno.html**). Go to the website or pick up a hypnosis spinning disk and stare at the center of the disk as it rotates. Just allow your entire consciousness to become totally aware of the spinning disk. Do this for about two minutes. Plan ahead and have a picture that you can turn your gaze towards immediately after your focus on the spinning disk. An amazing thing happens. Everyone loves this one, especially children, because the still picture suddenly comes alive. It is no longer a two-dimensional image; indeed, it becomes a three-dimensional, moving world.

In the wonderful film *What the Bleep Do We Know,* Candace Pert retells a story about the conquistadors and Montezuma. The story, an allegedly factual account, essentially states that when the Spanish galleons approached, they were invisible to the Aztec people. The reason was simply that the Aztec had never seen ships of this nature. When the Spanish approached the shore with their helmets on their heads, what the Aztec perceived were gods with golden helmets reflecting the sun as they walked on water. The Aztec welcomed them as gods, and of course everyone knows what happened. According to the story, it took several days of just staring at the water where the Spanish arrived for one of the Aztec sages to finally see the ships. Arguably, this story illustrates how we fail to see what we see, either because of psychological defense strategies and/or the inability to see what is not already in the mind to see.

A friend of mine, Professor William Guillory, has a model for this nature of perception. It is the so-called reality model and looks like the diagram on the next page.

William Guillory

The circularity of our perception becomes obvious after following the arrows in the diagram above. What does not become obvious to many is that the diagram represents the reality representation for most. In other words, most of us can see the circular looping but fail to recognize that it may apply to us.

In the next chapter we will look at defense strategies and once again make some of them an experience. Let me close this chapter with a few more illusions.

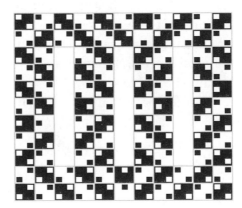

There are no curved lines in the diagram above.

There are only white circles between the black frames.

Read the following:

TΑΕ CΑT

This is a classic example of context perception. You probably read, "The Cat." But look closely. What is the difference between the H in the word *the* and the A in the word *cat*? Remember, we often make up the context and/or decide on an approved context.

The lines below are really equal in length.

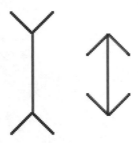

The photo below was used as a promotion photo for a seminar I taught in Malaysia, entitled "Change Without Thinking."

Did you notice the missing part of the face? Look closely at the space behind my right glasses lens. This photo was among a selection of photos I had had taken. Several months later, after many people had seen and approved the picture for PR purposes, someone noticed the defect behind the glasses. The brain is so used to filling in the blanks that most people do not even see this defect until it is pointed out to them.

If this sample of illusions has tricked you, then perhaps taking a closer look at your own expectations, beliefs, perceptions, or perceptual defenses, is in order.

Although optical illusions are widely circulated on the internet, most of the illusions used in this chapter were reprinted, with permission, from Antonio Zamora at **www.scientificpsychic.com**. If you enjoy cognitive illusions and would like to see some more, please visit my website, **www.choicesandillusions.com**.

*** ***

Be careful that victories do not carry
the seed of future defeats.
— Ralph W. Sockman

CHAPTER FOUR

Psychological Defense Mechanisms

A number of psychological defense mechanisms are designed to protect our self-image. Most people are at least aware of some of them. Those defense mechanisms known as perceptual defense mechanisms include the following:

Denial

As implied by its name, the mechanism of denial is simply one of denying. Often the denial occurs through projection, that is, projecting blame or fault onto another.

Fantasy formation

Fantasy formation creates a perceived reality out of fantasy. If motives cannot be satisfied in the objective external world, they may become a perceived reality in a dream world. Some psychologists suggest that the appeal for much of our entertainment is oriented to satisfying our fantasies for adventure, affection, and security perhaps not so vividly experienced otherwise.

Introjection

Introjection allows one to place blame on oneself. This self-directed blame or punishment defends against disappointment or disillusionment in another. For example, a child feels unworthy of the parent's attention because the parent pays no attention to the child.

Isolation

Isolation involves the avoidance of connecting associations to related ideas that produce anxiety. One set of data is isolated from an associated set: birth is isolated from death, war from mourning, nuclear arsenals from murderous horror, and so forth.

Projection
Projection allows one to project blame or responsibility onto another.

Regression
Regression is a mechanism common during serious illness. Essentially, one regresses to an earlier age, usually as a dependent, when one felt safe and comfortable. The individual usually returns to an earlier state of development where someone else assumed responsibility and where fewer, simpler, and more primitive goals existed.

Repression
Generally repression censors or prohibits memories, associations, and adjustments from conscious awareness. Like an invisible filter, this mechanism prevents the conscious mind from "seeing" painful memories and "stymied" motives. Personal experiences ranging from embarrassment to cruelty are often subject to the lens of repression.

Sublimation
Sublimation redirects basic drive mechanisms. Sublimation is simply the substitution of acceptable behavior to satisfy basic motives that might be met equally well in a primitive sense by some form of unacceptable social behavior. Aggression motives, for instance, are often met by sports activities. The process of sublimation is to find avenues in which basic motives may be satisfied in a manner acceptable to the individuals and to society.

In addition to these eight mechanisms, several miscellaneous escapes and defenses are considered by some theorists as contributing to the basic perceptual defenses, which show us only what we want to see about ourselves and the world around us. Several mechanisms can function at one time; in that case, the boundaries overlap, making it difficult to differentiate between the mechanisms.

**Basic perceptual defenses show each of us
only what we want to see about
ourselves and about the world around us.**

Repeated experiments have adequately demonstrated that the conscious mind is not a necessary part of information processing. In fact, the unconscious can and quite frequently does operate without the conscious, or at least is unknown to it. Freud once put it this way, "The most complicated achievements of thought are possible without the assistance of consciousness."

With this background we're ready to take a look at an example. Let me first introduce what you are about to see and warn you that some of the images are for adults, not for children. Several years ago an anonymous individual sent me an advertising training manual after reading my book *Subliminal Learning*. The manual described in very sophisticated terms the reason for embedding sexual taboos in advertising and provided the graphic example that I will show you. The bottom line to all the psychobabble is this: The sexual embeds are not consciously recognized due to perceptual mechanisms, but the result tends to increase product recognition because of increased dwell time (the time taken to view the ad or even to take the second glance before one turns the page). Judge for yourself now.

What follows first is the finished advertisement. Next you will see the artist's rendition made before setting a real model and props in place for a photo session designed to replicate the artist's portrayal. Next you will see the same image, but this time with the embeds outlined so they cannot be missed. Finally, you will see the outlined embeds alone.

I have intentionally used four separate pages in this book to prevent visual clues giving away the embeds early. Please take a moment to study the first two pages before viewing the embeds closer. (To see these illustrations in full color, go to **www.choicesandillusions.com**.)

The advertisement:

The artist's original conceptualization:

Close-up outlining the sexual and taboo embeds:

The outline of the embeds alone:

Once these embeds are pointed out, they are hard to miss, yet they are almost impossible to see when they have not been pointed out. In part this is due to various defense mechanisms—who wants to be accused of having a dirty mind? However, the most important factor here is that although this information went right beneath your conscious level of perception, it did not get past your subconscious level of perception. Advertisers use subliminals in this way to get you to take a greater interest in their ads, but that is not the focus of our attention now. Our purpose is to be aware of just how much information and technology are used to influence our beliefs, preferences, and choices.

Next we'll examine subliminal information processing. I will attempt to separate out the fact from the fiction and expose the so-called controversy. We will look at the varying definitions and the most current research findings.

**Much of the information you have processed in your
lifetime has been information that has passed beneath
your conscious sentry, or recognition.**

Subliminal information processing (or information processing
without awareness, as I prefer to call it) becomes particularly relevant
to our purpose for two reasons. First, much of the information you
have processed in your lifetime has been information that passed
beneath your conscious sentry, or recognition. Second, it is potentially a very useful tool for changing self-talk and thereby affecting
expectation, self-limiting beliefs, and so forth. But I'm getting ahead
of myself. It is important to know that a number of other mechanics
can conceal information from conscious awareness. Indeed, one of
the most interesting to me is how stress, distress, and trauma can
virtually hide experience from the conscious mind.

For years I practiced criminalistics, and one of my tools was
forensic hypnosis. I will never forget receiving a phone call one
evening from a local police department. There had been an armed
robbery involving a night deposit by a local theater manager. The
manager was able to tell authorities only that a "big gun" was pushed
into his face, as he was about to pass the money from the driver's side
of his vehicle into the night deposit drawer. The manager surrendered
the money and remained still as instructed for several minutes until
the thief escaped. Under hypnosis this same manager was able to tell
us in detail about the automobile used by the perpetrators. As it turned
out, this manager had formerly been a manager for Hertz and knew
automobiles very well. He had seen the car for a brief instant in his
rear-view mirror, as the dome light went on when it pulled in behind
him and the gunman jumped from the car while the driver waited
for a quick getaway. Under hypnosis, the theater manager provided
a complete description of both men, the automobile, and even a
partial license plate. The money was recovered, and the suspects were
apprehended within a few hours.

Even under the influence of drugs and alcohol, the subconscious
remembers. One case I was involved with proved this to me. I was

asked to run a lie-detection test and do forensic hypnosis on a young man incarcerated in the state prison for the murder of his mother. He claimed that he confessed to the crime only because of duress and promises of no prison time. He passed the lie-detection test, but that did not necessarily mean anything to me. During hypnosis, however, he was able to provide vivid details regarding his whereabouts at the time of the crime—details that included hiding in the park from police while they searched the trash on an unrelated matter. The time of the homicide, a rather brutal one involving a sex crime as well, made it impossible for this young man to be where he said he was and also to be the perpetrator. The information he had could not have been obtained from any of his sources. The police log and other sources confirmed the information, and in a new hearing he was acquitted. On the evening in question, he had been using drugs and alcohol and had no conscious recollection of anything between leaving a party and finding his mother's body, whereupon he phoned law enforcement. Without the aid of hypnosis, he would still be serving time.

Numerous mechanics underlie our perception, or at least our awareness of what we perceive. That is the important point. If all of the information we process, including the so-called no/don'ts we are typically raised under and all of the negative input we receive, both explicit and implied, and all of this information remains in our subconscious minds, it is no wonder that our thinking and our choices can seem so predisposed. The fact is, we *are* predisposed, and that is the crux of the matter.

Let us now look further at subliminal information processing before constructing a model of the mind.

*** ***

A certain amount of opposition is of great help
to a man. Kites rise against, not with, the wind.

— John Neal

CHAPTER FIVE

Information Processing Without Awareness

In the early 1980s I heard that the Los Angeles Police Department had experimented with subliminal programs for a terrorist abduction scenario as part of their preparation for the Olympic games to be hosted in L.A. The idea was a simple one. Because so much time is typically spent in negotiations over the phone, the subliminal messages would suggest illness. The masking sound was supposedly that of a furnace, or what is known as pink noise. I was told that the police department tested this program and then suspended it after three days because it was dehydrating cadets. I have never been able to either find confirmation or denial for this report, so I don't honestly know if it was done or not. What I do know is the story was the beginning of my interest in subliminal communication.

My business at the time was criminalistics. I owned an agency that, among other things, ran several hundred lie-detection tests a year. One of the problems encountered in deception testing is known as "inconclusives." That is, the charts are not clear enough to say with confidence that deception is indicated or that the test is nondeceptive. Inconclusives are generally the product of poor test structure and pre-interview techniques or, more commonly, counter-measures or situational stress. The long and the short of it goes this way. Honest persons are so nervous about the test results that their stress spills across all questions in such a way as to lower the net differential between relevant questions and pre-stressed, control, or irrelevant questions. Dishonest persons employ some countermeasure like the proverbial tack in the shoe and selectively administer discomfort to themselves during relevant questions, again possibly skewing the differential. I simply thought how wonderful it would be to use a subliminal program to ease the situational stress for the honest and to heighten it for those who intended to deceive.

To make a long story short, I decided to find out more about subliminal communication. The literature even then was rather robust with research demonstrating the efficacy of subliminal communication. Unfortunately for me, most of the work employed visual subliminal methods, like the tachistoscope, which simply would not work in my intended application. The remaining literature dealt with audio but under tightly controlled conditions in which hearing tests for individual thresholds of conscious perception were conducted first and the ambient background noise was controlled so as not to add noise to signal strength ratios. However, a number of anecdotal reports ranged from curbing shoplifting to eliminating fainting while waiting for medical procedures. Most of the anecdotal evidence that I came across had something to do with the "Becker Black Box."

As with many others, my early knowledge regarding subliminal this and that arose from the popular media. There were the infamous cola and popcorn claims made by James Vicary, who claimed to increase concession sales by flashing such things as "hungry—eat popcorn" on the face of Kim Novak during the showing of the movie *Picnic.* Contrary to popular opinion, this may have never happened. Vicary owned another business and intended to sell a subliminal projector to theaters around the country. When Congress called Vicary to testify regarding the alleged "popcorn" messages, he denied doing so. We do know that he had the capability. The Congressional hearings in 1984 regarding subliminal communication and the outrage of the American public, the entire Orwellian fear mentality of the time, may have induced him to deny doing such a thing. (For more information, see my book *Thinking Without Thinking*).

Books by Norman Cousins and Vance Packard shouted out fear messages regarding the power of subliminal communication. Cousins termed this technology potentially the most dangerous ever developed. Packard, in *Hidden Persuaders,* spoke of how it could be used to manipulate the public. Then along came Wilson Brian Keyes, whose books pictorially illustrated the use of subliminal messages in everything from menus to Playboy advertisements. The alarmed public demanded something be done to protect them from this invasion of their minds. There were hearings and articles, but in the end no laws were passed to prevent its use. (For more detail, see my books *Thinking Without Thinking* and *Subliminal Communication*.) In the United States the FCC did create a codification that is supposed to prevent the broadcast of subliminal messages. The unfortunate truth of the matter is that more than one case has been taken to the FCC and no penalties have ever been imposed. Even the now infamous "RATS" ad that appeared on television during the Bush/Gore presidential campaign failed to move the FCC to do anything more than condemn. You may recall that in this advertisement, the subliminal message bolded above Mr. Gore's head was "RATS," taken from the small print DemocRATS. The Democrats cried foul, and the people behind the Bush advertisement first asserted "accident" and then admitted intention, but it was just a joke, not meant to be taken seriously.

Another point worth noting regarding legislation has to do with legislation proposed in the state of Utah. This legislation would not have made the use of subliminal information illegal; it would simply have required informed consent. So, if a retailer wished to use subliminal anti-theft messages, that would be fine—provided the retailer published the fact that such messages were used and made the actual affirmations available upon request. The reason for the latter was simply due to some of the so-called anti-theft messages that I had seen. For example, a message such as "Buying is honest" is also a motivational message, not just an anti-theft message. The legislation was approved by the committee after a veritable who's-who in the advertising world showed up in Utah to oppose it. The opposition loudly asserted that the law was unnecessary because no one used subliminal messages and that they would not do so simply because subliminals did not work. Although the committee approved the proposed law, it never went to the floor for a vote.

**To this day, no legislation protects
the consumer from subliminal manipulation.**

A representative of a foreign politician contacted my office regarding subliminal advertising. I advised against it unless it was done with full disclosure. For example, informing the public that you were using a subliminal message to get out the vote might attract favorable attention to both the politician and the campaign. On the other hand, it could backfire. Either way, if used it would in all probability be discovered.

Back to my story, then. Because many companies were offering subliminal tapes, I phoned a number of them. I explained who I was and asked how they made their tapes. You might have thought I was asking for the secret recipe for Coca-Cola. In my opinion, companies that made so-called scientific claims were obligated to provide at least some information regarding the nature of how they prepared a program that supposedly altered behavior. No one was forthcoming. Eventually I purchased some programs and sent them to Audio Forensic Laboratories in California for analysis. When I received the report, I knew why the matter was such a secret. The bottom line was that there were no subliminal messages on the tapes—any of them—at least, there was no recoverable verbal content of any kind.

It was clear that for a stimulus to affect someone, there must be sufficient signal strength. Subtract the signal strength, and everything became about as subliminal as something being said a mile away. For some this may have been satisfactory because, after all, the mind was magical and it could extract verbal messages from the ether. This notion did not work for me, however. So I went back to the drawing board.

Reviewing the literature again, I found quite a bit of good audio work on what is called shadowing, or dichotic listening, experiments. Essentially, this type of work masks one message with another. One ear may receive random numbers for a period while the other perceives a partial story, then the partial story switches to the numbers ear and the numbers switch to the story ear. Subjects normally report hearing the story and fail to report the numbers. Sometimes random words are presented to one ear and a partial story to the other. The brain selects the words it needs to complete, or fill in, the story, which is simultaneously delivered to the opposite ear. See the following illustration.

A typical shadowing task. The messages are presented simultaneously to the left and right ears, and the subject attempts to shadow one ear.

Here the subject follows the meaningful message as it moves from one ear to the other.

Now I must take a step or two backwards. I was familiar with something called "back masking," and a sound engineer for a couple of major artists had told me that he personally mixed backward messages into their songs. I was also convinced that children mixing up 5's and S's by writing them backwards, as so very many seem to do, were simply correcting for some mirrored image in the mind. Further, the holographic models put forth by such researchers as Karl Pribram and David Bohm had provided a simple mechanic by which this speech reversal, or mirroring, was accomplished. I have referred to this mirroring model as the MIP method, or Mirror Imaging Paradigm, in my books on subliminal information. As you may recall, Karl Pribram, the noted neuroscientist, and David Bohm, the Nobel Prize–winning physicist, advanced the theory that the brain stores information holographically. That is, it stores information across all of the brain. According to this theory, every cell carries information, or more specifically, memories, like a tiny piece of holographic film. (When a film plate catches a holographic image, the plate can be cut into many pieces, but when light is shined through any of the pieces, the contents of the entire plate are visible. In other words, unlike a picture cut into several pieces, perhaps forming a puzzle, every fragment of the holographic film contains the entire image).

The right hemisphere is the spatial, creative, and nonlinear hemisphere; the left hemisphere is subject to the rules of language, logic, and linear thinking.

Brain hemispheric specialization theories argue that the right hemisphere, for typical right-handed people, is the spatial, creative, and nonlinear hemisphere; whereas the left hemisphere is subject to the rules of language, logic, and linear thinking. The right hemisphere is also the seat of the unconscious or subconscious. Using simple deductive reasoning, it occurred to me that the right hemisphere probably acquired language first, because its development by way of specialization precedes the left. (Infants first perceive dark and light, then shapes, and so forth). If this were the case, and since hard research has proven that memory is indeed stored across all of the brain,[11] then word representations in an oversimplified representation may look like the illustration below.

I added this all up, and the light dawned. What if I were to mask forward speech with reverse speech? Would this confuse the mind enough for it to fail to consciously discriminate the speech? You see, hemispheric specialization explained the famous Stroop Effect, in my view. Because one hemisphere entertained more than the other such things as space and color while the other hemisphere dealt with the rules of language, logic, and so forth, when a person is called upon to integrate the two, there is a noticeable failure. For those of you unfamiliar with the Stroop Test, this is where the names of various colors are printed in colors that to do not correspond with the name of the color. For example, the word *yellow* would be printed in green, the word *blue* printed in red, and so forth. (If you would like to try this test for yourself, please go to **www.choicesandillusions.com**.)

What most people find is that there is substantial interference between the spelling of the word and the color of the typeface. What should be a simple task becomes quite difficult. Combining this information, I decided to deliver both forward speech and reverse speech and disguise it with a soundtrack, ocean with birds, or ocean with music. In doing so, I found that a person's ability to discriminate the speech was almost entirely lost. In time, this method became known as the Taylor Method, and I patented this method, together with some other claims, totaling 105 in all. (This technology is known as InnerTalk today.) When I ran studies, at least everyone would be able to see exactly how we did things by simply viewing the patent and, as with all good science, test or replicate my findings.

All right, I had a method. And by the way, unknown to me at the time, another researcher by the name of David Oates was simultaneously working on reverse speech. There is little doubt today that some children process language in reverse. (You might want to visit his website, **www.reversespeech.com**, and listen for yourself). We often mistake as gibberish the speech of small children in the phase of speech development where the child looks you right in the eye and says something that is not goo-goo gaga but you don't understand what the child is saying. Yet, when such speech is played backwards, it is meaningful speech, such as "Daddy, help!" What is more, various law enforcement agencies have learned, as I did, that reversing the answers in a statement may reveal some interesting information. This first happened to me when I was manually reversing a recording made at 7–IPS to replay it at 15/16–IPS through a Psychological Stress Evaluator, a method of truth verification. As I manually turned the spool on my Uher recorder, the forward answer "no" became "liar." This astounded me, especially when the charts agreed that deception was present. A confession taken later verified that the subject was indeed lying. How was this possible? Well, the exact mechanics are not known. What has been verified, though, is that reverse speech can add information, refute statements, and often do even more. In one criminal case, for example, statements that dealt with an armed robbery actually revealed the location of the hidden money when they were slowed down and played in reverse. As with the so-called Freudian slip, apparently the subconscious needs to get in its proverbial two bits' worth as well.

My new method gave rise to the detection of occasional speech sounds, such as someone talking softly, but the words were not consciously discriminated. What message would give rise to minimizing distress in a detection of deception examination unless the subject intended to practice deception—and then have the reverse effect? This was not easy, but in the end I elected to use two components: the statement "The truth shall set you free" and the entire 23rd Psalm. (The 23rd Psalm was used by many of our prisoners of war during WWII and Korea, according to their reports, to assuage the anxiety and stress of capture.) The results astonished me. Not only did inconclusives disappear but confession rates soared. In fact, there were times I thought of saying, "Stop, don't tell me yet—I get paid by the hour."

I reported my findings to some of the local law enforcement agencies and heard back that the prosecutor did not think our using this technology was such a good idea, so we stopped. Still, now that I knew this technology could work in a lie detection scenario, I wondered about using it to rehabilitate prison inmates. A friend of mine from the Utah State Prison staff, Lee Liston, approached me with the initial idea, and we went to work on setting up a rather extensive study. We called upon another friend, Dr. Charles McCusker, a psychometric specialist, and set up a study using the Minnesota Multiphasic Personality Inventory (MMPI), which is the clinical instrument most often used to provide an objective measure of personality. It is employed quite often in court cases and is generally deemed the most reliable instrument for personality assessment.

Our study used prison inmates who volunteered for the study. They were divided into three groups: an experimental group that would receive the messages designed to lower hostility and aggression and improve chances at rehabilitation (interrupt the recidivism rate), a placebo group that would listen to the sounds of the ocean without messages, and a control group that would do nothing. The study was to take place over thirty days with the inmate volunteers listening to the programs a minimum of one hour a day every day.

The MMPI was administered using a modified version developed for the incarcerated environment, known as the Fowler Lens. The MMPI was used first to determine a so-called common denominator. The results of the MMPI yielded no real surprises, as there were high scores in both self and social alienation. We decided to use the Thurstone Temperament schedule before and after the test to determine what effect our InnerTalk program had. However, I was still faced with the question, "What do we say to the inmates?"

It's okay to do better than Daddy.

Mommy and I are one.

The research literature had only two magic messages. The work of Lloyd Silverman at New York State demonstrated that the message "It's okay to do better than Daddy" had remarkable results in a variety of domains, and the "Mommy and I are one" message seemed to have universal power, from improving dart-throwing ability to reducing symptoms of schizophrenia. Silverman theorized that Freudian complexes were often sublimated in adaptive ways that could lead to schisms in the psyche, which led him to the subliminal message, "Mommy and I are one."[12] My own work (as I have set out in my other books) suggests that this "Mommy" is not our actual physical mother but rather the universal archetype of motherhood, namely the womb. The womb—whether of a mother or of nature, the planet, the living consciousness known as Gaia—is a place of sanctuary. Indeed, Silverman's own work showed that the message had no effect if the subject was conscious of its presence. "How wonderful," I thought in reviewing this literature. "I somehow don't think the 'Mommy' message is quite enough with our prison population." So what message or messages should be used on the program?

**Researchers at Boston University's Center for Brain
and Memory have pinpointed the mechanism
that makes subliminal learning work.**

It was time to speak with the inmates and let them tell us what should be on the program. What we discovered changed my life and could change yours. In the next chapter, we will review this information, and I will again attempt to make it personal with some stories and experiential material. In chapters to come, I will share other experiences and offer my opinions on what is behind some of the misconceptions regarding subliminal communication. It is worth noting that today there is little controversy. Even the neurological mechanism for subliminal learning has been identified. In May 2005 a team of researchers led by Takeo Watanabe of Boston University's Center for Brain and Memory announced that "his team had pinpointed the mechanism that makes subliminal learning work." [13]

*** ***

You have powers you never dreamed of.
You can do things you never thought you could.
There are no limitations in what you can do except
the limitations of your own mind.
— Darwin P. Kingsley

CHAPTER SIX

A Simple Model of Mind and Behavior

When I have spoken to inmates, they all have stories and persons or events on which to blame their life errors. In lectures, I have often summed up their attitudes this way: "Ah, but for the grace of God, you would be where I am today. My mother was a prostitute, and my daddy an alcoholic. The neighbor boy hung heroin on me when I was 12." Et cetera, et cetera, et cetera. In other words, their situation is not their fault. Even when their stories are false or greatly exaggerated, it still is not their fault. They all have someone or something to blame. They would seek to gain understanding and even sympathy with their life stories. Not that some of the stories are not touching, but my point is that the function of blame essentially removed their responsibility through such rationalizations as "What would you have done?" or "Maybe it was wrong, but what else could I do?" Their so-called choices are framed in experience much like those in our flowerpot story.

The inmates generally have a compensation mechanism that differs from the compensation mechanisms of people in society. Remember the high scores in social- and self-alienation. Typically, the person with low self-esteem tends to adapt by thinking of others as better. This was not necessarily true in our inmate population. Many of them had compensated this way: "If I'm no good, you're no good. Do unto others before they do unto you. Don't get even; get 'evener'."

For the record, I have discovered that what I am about to share with you works everywhere. It worked in the prison system, and it works in hospice centers. It works with professional elite athletes, Fortune 500 types, small children, and everyone in between. It works in Germany, China, Malaysia, Singapore, Mexico, Canada, India, England, Ireland, and more. I know it works there because we have distributors and customers, as well as studies, coming from these areas. I am convinced it works everywhere, in every language, on all human beings.

What, then, to put on the prison subliminal program? It should be obvious, but allow me to digress for a moment. There are two ways to be tied up in the world. In one way, another person binds you. In the other way, you choose to hold onto a tiny thread attached to anything and refuse either to let go or pull hard enough to break the thread. You might feel like you're walking around, but as soon as you reach the thread's end, you turn and retreat. It's interesting that this is how elephants are trained. Tying elephants when they are very young with large chains causes the elephants to soon learn they are attached and if they try to run, the ground will suddenly be jerked out from under them and they will fall and hurt themselves. When the elephants are full-grown and could easily snap the chain, they are content tied only with a small rope. They choose—if you can use that word in this context—not to test the boundary.

Similarly, blame is a bind—pure and simple, it ties you up!

As long as we blame, we effectively rob ourselves of our own empowerment. After all, if it's not my fault, then there is nothing I can do about it. "The world sucks and then you die" attitude, the "it's not my fault" approach, and so forth, strip individuals of the power to effect their own world. The net result, as Robert Laing so eloquently says in *Politics of Experience,* is:

> The condition of alienation, of being asleep, of being unconscious, of being out of one's mind, is the condition of the normal man.
>
> Society highly values its normal man. It educates children to lose themselves and to become absurd, and thus to be normal.

Normal men have killed perhaps 100,000,000 of their fellow men in the last fifty years . . .

We are not able even to think adequately about the behavior that is at the annihilating edge. But what we think is less than what we know; what we know is less than what we love; what we love is so much less than what there is. And to that precise extent we are so much less than what we are.

As long as we blame, we effectively rob ourselves of our own empowerment.

Now, let us build a model and see if we can find the gears and tumblers that cause all of this non-sense to seem sensical. In the figure below, the circle represents the mind.

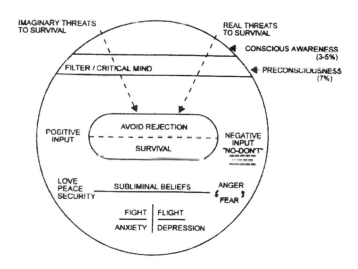

MODEL OF SUBLIMINAL PROGRAMMING

According to the notion that we use 10 percent or less of our brain/mind, our model shows 3 percent is conscious awareness at any given time; 7 percent or so is preconscious, or that part of our mind that accesses, say, the verse to a favorite song that we do not carry around full-time in our conscious mind; and the remaining 90 percent is untapped resources and our subconscious or unconscious. Here I am using subconscious and unconscious synonymously despite being fully aware there is a sharp demarcation between the two in the psychological literature.

At the bottom of the diagram you find fight/flight over anxiety/depression. In modern man, fight has become anxiety (preparedness to fight, a heightened state of arousal) and depression has replaced flight. In fact, in cases of chronic depression, the subjects have fled inward so much so that they often withdraw almost completely from the outer world.

Notice that above the circle are indicated two forms of stimuli. Real stimuli might be that old saber tooth tiger or a 357 Magnum held to our head. Now why the synthetic stimulus? Synthetic here refers to a stimulus that is not life threatening, as with a real stimulus, but to which we respond as though it were. In other words, when our bodies go to the budget we identified earlier as defense, the old anxiety and/or depression kick in. Whether the stimulus is real or imagined (synthetic), our bodies respond chemically. For many that synthetic stimulus can be a look from their employer, a word from their significant other, a letter in the mail making some demand, even someone cutting in front and "flipping them off" during rush hour traffic. Because the synthetic stimuli are what most of us live with, it is fair to ask, What makes these stimuli capable of triggering a fight/flight, anxiety/depression response?

Let us look again at our model. We see rejection avoidance over survival. It would appear that our need to be accepted, respected, and so forth is weighted as equal or nearly equal to our drive to survive. A basic human need is acceptance. Whether this is to accommodate the so-called basic drives covered earlier or for some other reason is not so clear—but the fact is, we do all need to be accepted and loved. Something intrinsic is threatened when we are cut off in traffic or meet with disdain and rejection from another human being, particularly one who has power of some kind over us.

What is also interesting about this synthetic stimulus is that it is not the same for all of us. A stressful stimulus to some is a sought-after stimulus for others. One factor is universal, and that follows in a construct model of the mind. Look again at our model. Beneath the rejection/survival is something I have labeled "subliminal beliefs." Our subconscious beliefs, some of which we know and some we do not, create a sort of calculus. Imagine a measuring stick with -10 on one end and +10 on the other. At one end would be -10 units of pleasure, which becomes 10 units of pain, and the other end, 10 units of pleasure. Jeremy Benthom called this a Hedonic Calculus.[14] Using this measurement, we can scale belief from a point of love/peace/security to anger/fear. On opposite ends of the line in our model representing these unconscious, or subliminal, beliefs, we find a scale that can be thought of this way. Most human beings seek to feel loved and secure, and much behavior is built around avoiding rejection. When our beliefs are threatened, the result moves the scale towards anger and fear.

In the typical parenting/peer-related maturation process, each of us receives a quantity of input. Some of it is positive, but most is negative. All the no/don'ts and self-limiting beliefs are posited here in our subliminal beliefs. Every time we have been told we are stupid, unattractive, fat or skinny, not old enough, not smart enough, and so forth, it has been recorded in our subconscious mind. These no/don'ts combined with the "shoulds" and "oughts" form the mold for our beliefs. Among them are those trainings that have been acquired from our entertainment, like the right to get even. All of this non-sense becomes what we believe—our reality, which anchors our self-definition and experience and serves as a loop to reinforce our beliefs. Our language, experience, and feedback have been programmed without our conscious awareness or agreement.

Years ago I created a couple of anagrams for anger and fear. They are circular. Anger=A Nasty Getting Even Response. Fear=For Every Anger Response. So, for every anger response, there is a nasty getting even response. There is no such thing as anger without fear. Some of the so-called tough guys in the world should get this—there is no such thing as anger without a fear attached!

For Every Anger Response
there is
A Nasty Getting Even Response.

What is the fear, you might ask? The fear can be any number of things. It can vary from "you took something from me," including our space in the queue during rush hour traffic (acceptance/respect), to "you don't believe the same way I do," which again is oriented toward avoidance of rejection.

What I discovered with the prison inmates was the ability to displace responsibility. A function not shown in our model is known as blame. Blame is the way we escape responsibility, and it too is defined by our culture. To justify irrational behavior, thoughts, and so forth, even if we fail to recognize the irrational nature of it all, we blame. The inmates blamed. It was not their fault, and you should understand that. The actual facts might be quite different—not that some of this or that negativity wasn't present—but many people face the same obstacles and make entirely different choices from criminality.

I like to think of obstacles as opportunities. Why not, after all? It is much more pragmatic to deal with challenges in a positive manner than in a negative one, if for no other reason than health and personal well-being—the old body chemicals, remember? Indeed, let me share a real pragmatic viewpoint with you. I have learned to approach life with an attitude of gratitude. Long before that became a popular new idea, and largely from my own research and work such as that with the inmate prison population, I discovered that an antidote to negativity could be had by just changing the way I defined certain things. So, when someone or something happens that might produce stress, anger, and so forth, I invoke this little phrase:

"I can't wait to see what good happens from this."

I choose to look at the world as providing everything I need right now. I choose to think that everything that comes to me does so for some good. Finding that good might not always be so easy, but thinking this way transforms the poison that might otherwise accumulate in my body, such as cortisol. Cortisol is a chemical stored in the body as a result of stress. Anger and fear, blame and shame are stressors that generate cortisol. Cortisol kills, literally. It has been linked to early aging and various diseases as well as brain degeneration. It is not something any rational person really wants to create, let alone save.

So with my new attitude, I pulled into my office parking lot one bright summer morning. As I passed a video store in the same strip mall, a driver suddenly backed from his parking stall into the side of my new car. Smash! My first thought was not my preferred thought, but I quickly adjusted and rather snidely said aloud to myself, "I can't wait to see what good comes from this!"

The driver of the car that slammed into me jumped from his vehicle, yelling obscenities. He claimed that I had hidden behind his old beat-up jalopy just so he would hit me. *Right,* I thought. *I hid my new Cadillac behind your junk heap just so you could hit me.* I only smiled at the older man and his cussing. As it happened, law-enforcement officers were in the parking lot and saw the entire incident. They too got an ear full of how I had hid behind the jalopy just so I could get hit. It was sad—except that it was funny. This older gentleman had no insurance or driver's license. That didn't matter to me because my insurance policy covered uninsured motorists. Well, the long and the short of it is my car was fixed as good as new, my body chemicals were those of laughter, although I did not laugh at the man, and his body chemicals—well, you get the picture. The pure pragmatist in me saved who knows how much cortisol from my system and, as with the flowerpot, what good would getting mad have done anyway?

Back to our prison inmates. Their mechanism, blame, essentially displaced their personal responsibility. Further, unlike most people, their self-esteem social issues gave rise to a philosophy that can be stated this way: "If I'm no good, then you aren't either." This is an inverted form of the "I'm okay, you're okay" idea. As such, a sort of "Do unto others before they do unto you" credo existed, even if they did not overtly recognize it.

Here was our clue—now we could plan what to say on our subliminal program. We had to undo the blame game. As I mentioned earlier, there are essentially two ways to be tied up in the world. Someone can physically bind you or you can hold onto some thread and refuse to pull it hard enough to break it, and you are just as tethered as if you were actually tied. Holding onto blame is the same as being tied up. Until blame is released, there is nothing you can do about anything, because, after all, it's not your fault. If it is not your fault, then how can anyone, including you, expect you to take responsibility for the issue? If you are not responsible, then you are not empowered to make changes. In other words, the blame game disempowers—directly. Indeed, to the precise extent we blame anything or anyone, we surrender our empowerment franchise.

Bad-luck fortune-cookie collectors.

Interestingly, however, there are those who cling to their "right" to blame. I have a friend in South Africa who is a lie-detection examiner. He has a model I like. He calls it something else, but we'll call it the "bad-luck fortune cookies" game. So, this is the story of these special cookie collectors. They go through life collecting all the cookies they can. Riding on the escalator of life, they will even jump high in the air to catch one, just so they can put it in their backpack of life experience and share it later. And share they do. Each evening, whether at home or in the pub, on the telephone or on e-mail, they tell their friends all about the cookies of the day. These sharings go like this:

> *First Person:* "Do you know what happened to me today? The clerk in the gas and grocery would not take my credit card because I left my purse at work with my identification in it; and she knows me. Heck, she sees me nearly every day—but she is a real grouch anyway."

Second Person: "That sucks, but do you know what my boss said to me today? He informed me that I was always late from lunch and told me in no uncertain terms that I would either be on time or lose my job. He knows that the traffic is horrible at lunch, and he's always gone more than an hour. I should just tell him to stuff it!"

Third Person: "Your day was nearly as bad as mine. I had a damn cop stop me for nearly nothing. Everyone in traffic was changing lanes, and just because I cut in front of him, he gave me a ticket. That's my third one this year, and my insurance costs are going to go through the roof as a result. These damn cops should be out catching criminals, not honest tax-paying citizens."

First Person: "Life sucks. Is your husband still being a jerk? Oh, but you know, speaking of insurance rates, my insurance company canceled my insurance just because I was late with their payment. Then that blankity blank that ran into me led to a fine for my not having insurance. And on top of that, they blamed me for the accident, and it wasn't my fault!"

By now you get the idea. These people gather to share their cookie stories, and that is largely what their social life is all about. If you want to have some fun, step up to the cookie keepers and point out how wonderful life is. You might even explain the blame game and cookie-keeper philosophy, but make sure you have a plan for a quick retreat.

Cookie keepers choose, whether or not they want to admit it, to hold tightly to the blame game. An otherwise productive and joyful life is thrown away in exchange for the "Don't you feel sorry for me?" exchanges. That is another part of the cookie keeper game. To belong to their group, you must be willing to be understanding and sympathetic. It's okay to top the cookie of another with a more unpleasant cookie of your own but not if you fail to recognize the poor, picked-on nature of the other cookie keeper.

A dear friend of mine grew up in a codependent family relationship, one of those Melody Beattie so aptly defines in her books such as *Codependent No More*. It's the relationship most of us know something about, for we have heard many of those conditional statements growing up. They are ones that go like this: "If you loved me, you would ____. If you had any respect for me, you would not _____. I did this for you, is it too much to expect _____ from you? I think if you cared about me, you would_____." And so forth. You fill in the blanks. Beattie sets out several criteria for recognizing codependence. "Codependents are the people who consistently, and with a great deal of effort and energy, try to force things to happen," she says. She continues:

> "We control in the name of love. We do it because we're 'only trying to help.' We do it because we know best how things should go and how people should behave. We do it because we're right and they're wrong. We control because we're afraid not to do it. We do it because we don't know what else to do. We do it to stop the pain. We control because we think we have to. We control because we don't think. We control because controlling is all we can think about. Ultimately we may control because that's the way we've always done things. Tyrannical and dominating, some rule with an iron hand. . . . Others do their duty behind a costume of sweetness and niceties, secretly going about their business—**other people's business.**"

Two of the keystone elements in all of this codependency is, according to Beattie, "Suffering people's consequences for them" and "Solving people's problems for them." In other words, there is a real quid pro quo in cookie sharing, and it too is at least somewhat based on codependent patterns.

My friend gave up her codependent behavior and threw all of her cookies away. She chose to become self-empowered and has made wonderful strides in the process. If you asked her, she would tell you life is a miracle, and she is very happy today. Still, her sister, with whom she has always been very close, has not budged. Her sister carries all the cookies she can and spends nearly every moment sharing them. Despite soft approaches at trying to turn on a light in the sister's head, my friend now finds herself in that place where many who refuse to play these games eventually arrive. It is hard to change when those you love the most are fixed in ways that steal your power. My friend has decided that the next time her sister plays the blame game, she will say something to end this behavior. You see, when you stop saving your cookies and get on with taking responsibility for everything in your life, your life improves. When that happens, you lose any and all desire to be a cookie keeper.

**Self-responsibility means taking responsibility
for everything in your life, even those events or people that
do not in any way seem to be your problem or responsibility.**

Often the people that most antagonize us are the ones we need most to teach us what we want to learn. My mother used to say, "Birds of a feather flock together." Call it that, or call it simple attraction, anger attracts anger, hostility attracts hostility, love attracts love, and so forth. As I mentioned earlier, what we resist we tend to become. When we see something in someone we do not like, we need to be careful, for often they are mirrors of ourselves. What we dislike in them is likely to be a behavior of our own. When we are alert to this, it's quite easy to do something remarkable, something that truly changes your own reality. Let me digress a minute.

When I lived in Las Vegas, Nevada, my local post office was always jammed with patrons. They all seemed in a hurry, and the clerks were absolutely rude. Many times heated arguments erupted between patrons and staff. I decided to try a little experiment. "What would happen if I just smiled and beamed light to all of these people?" I thought.

Every day for at least two weeks when I stopped to pick up my mail, I did my best to focus light on all. One day the oldest and grouchiest of the postal clerks, whose line I was queued in, looked up and said, "Hello, Dr. Taylor." There was a smile on his face and in his voice. From that day forward, every clerk in the office spoke and smiled, laughed and joked with me. Everything had changed. They were still snippy with other patrons for a while, but the smile and light had paid off. Somehow, unconsciously even, they identified me with warmth and love. Within a few months this post office and its employees were as warm and friendly with everyone as any I have ever visited.

It is amazing what a little unconditional love can do. We all are capable of coaching or cheering on our friends and family, but when it comes to strangers, particularly those we think of as rude, it is often another matter. It doesn't have to be. This is just another way to do good deeds.

Again, self-responsible means taking responsibility for every-thing in your life. That does not mean you're in charge of your environment and in control of all the stimuli you encounter. It does mean that you're in charge of your own inner environment and you begin to make choices—true choices that are healthy and wise. The so-called bad luck is seen through a different lens. In fact, there's a story about luck that I like to tell because it illustrates well just how limited our judgments can be. First, however, to frame the story, let me tell you about one of my favorite country songs. The song titled "Unanswered Prayers" tells of a young man who falls in love with a girl in high school. He prays nightly that she will see him and love him in return. She marries another man, and years pass. He eventually meets a woman who turns out to be the real woman of his dreams. A few more years pass, and he receives an invitation to a high school reunion. At the reunion he sees the sweetheart who married another. She has aged early, is nasty and bitter, and in other ways is totally unattractive. He looks at his wife and says, "Thank God for unan-swered prayers!"

"Thank God for unanswered prayers!"

So here is the story.

An old rancher back in the Civil War days was just barely getting by. His wife had died giving birth to his only son, and he himself was somewhat crippled with arthritis. His son, therefore, did most the work around the ranch. Now, this rancher was a really nice man, and everyone in town liked him.

One day, the boy was out tilling the ground when lightning struck near the mules. The mules bolted, and the old harness could not hold them. The harness broke, and the mules ran off.

Without the mules, the rancher and his son would not be able to get their crops in, and they were barely making ends meet as it is was. The whole town turned out to commiserate. "Such bad luck" they said. But the old farmer said, "Good luck, bad luck; who knows?"

Good luck, bad luck; who knows?

The next day the mules came running home, and behind them came a whole herd of wild horses. The farmer and his son seized the opportunity because horses were worth a lot of money. Armies on both sides of the Civil War were paying a lot of money for horses. They ran outside and opened the corral gates. When the horses and mules were inside, they closed the gates.

This time the whole town came out to congratulate them. "Such good luck!" they said. But the farmer just said, "Good luck, bad luck; who knows?"

The next day the son went out to break the horses, as nobody would buy a horse he could not ride. However, the very first pony he mounted simply sunfished and switched over. This means that he went up facing west and came down facing east, and then reared completely over backwards. The boy was lucky he wasn't more seriously hurt, just a broken arm and collarbone. This time the whole town came out to say, "Such bad luck." The old farmer simply said, "Good luck, bad luck; who knows?"

The very next day the army marched through town and conscripted every able-bodied man. Of course they did not take the farmer's son, because his arm and collarbone were broken. The whole town turned out again: "Such good luck." The old farmer simply said, "Good luck, bad luck; who knows?"

The army was heading to Shiloh. Not many lived through that battle. You just never know what is good luck and what is bad luck. But when your bones are broken, you tend to think only of the pain, the inconvenience, the discomfort and so on.

I was first told this story many years ago. Recently I learned it was actually a Sufi story and that Jonathan Robinson wrote a poem based on it. That poem, titled "The Old Man," is a slightly different version of the story above. In honor of the true story, here is the poem:

Once long ago, there lived an old man.
He had no money. He had no plan.
All that he had was a horse oh so grand
and he and his horse lived off the land.

The King offered riches for this horse oh so fine,
"I'll give you money if you'll make your horse mine."
But the old man said, "My horse will not be sold.
He lives with me. He lives free and bold."

Then one day the horse was plain gone.
"The horse has been stolen," the townsfolk cried on.
The old man said, "Friends, don't look so sad,
Though the horse may be gone that may not be so bad."

"You foolish old man, look what you've done.
You had a fine horse and now you have none.
A curse it is and a curse it will be.
You shouldn't have let your horse wander free!"

The horse soon returned with others by its side.
There were twelve now of beauty and pride.
The townsfolk said, "Old man, you were right.
You are blessed to have horses of unearthly delight!"

"I have now 12 horses, yes, that is true,
But that does not mean I am blessed with them too.
It is too soon to judge; who knows what will be?
Try not to make stories from the little you see."

As it came to pass, the old man's only son
Tried riding a horse, just for fun.
Yet he broke both his legs while playing this game
And the townsfolk cried, "Oh, what a shame!"

The old man said, "Friends, don't speak so soon.
You hear just one note, yet you sing an entire tune.
Who's to say what the future may hold?
My son's legs are broken, but the future lies untold."

Soon there was a war, and the young men of town
Were all sent to fight and were shot down.
But the old man's son was saved from this plight.
He had broken his legs; he was forced not to fight.

And the townsfolk cried out, "Again you were right!"
But the old man replied, "Have you no sight?
Only God knows what is and will be.
To live and let live is to live and live free."

To live and let live is to live and live free.

Either way, poem or story, the moral is clear: What often appears to be bad luck simply is not. Most of us, if honest, have everything we need right now—and now is our only certainty. If we choose to live in "now" with a gratitude attitude, taking what comes to us as the old farmer might, we'd be happier and live longer, healthier lives. That is just a fact. Why would anyone choose otherwise?

Mankind is unique. We all have the ability to think about the future. What about tomorrow? What if_____? (You fill in the blank.) All this worry over possibilities that we might actually be creating because we worry over them. It is clear that there is no pragmatic value in keeping cookies, playing the blame game, or disenfranchising ourselves while poisoning our bodies with chemicals on account of so-called synthetic threats.

Before we leave the subject of "now," allow me to share two more stories with you. This one I heard years ago from a friend who did not know where it came from. It is about a Zen master who made it a habit at noontime to meditate while he walked in the gardens. On this particular day he became so engrossed in his meditation that he wandered far into the jungle, where he met a hungry tiger. Well, our Zen master did what any Zen master would do, which is to attend to the urgency of the moment. He fled as fast as he could with the hungry tiger in pursuit. Soon he came to the edge of a sheer cliff, but with a hungry tiger about to eat him, he jumped over the edge. On the way down he grabbed the only thing jutting out from the cliff, a small tree. There he hung on as he heard a roar from below. Now, there was a hungry tiger above and a hungry tiger below. Just then the small tree began to pull out of the ground. He looked to his right. Nothing. He looked below. Nothing. He looked to his left. A beautiful strawberry. He picked the strawberry, and it was the best fruit he'd eaten in his life.

I have told this story many times in seminars around the world. Sometimes I have added things that might go through the minds of many: "Oh, I love strawberries, but I'm allergic to them," or we might fret those last precious moments of "now" away in panic, fear, and blame, "Why me, God?"

There are as many divisible units in "now" as there are in infinity, mathematically speaking. Living fully in the moment allows us to enjoy life with awe. The moral of the story is, look for the strawberries.

Look for the strawberries!

After I told this story to an audience in Malaysia, a fellow approached me during a break and asked if I knew the entire story.

"I thought that was the entire story."

"No," he said. "Would you like to know it?"

We sat down and had coffee while he related the story that he said comes from Paramahansa Yogananda. It seems that the Zen master, when confronted with the tigers, was actually hanging from a small apple tree while mice were digging away the light soil that the tree was rooted in. The story cuts away to a picture of the event hanging in a gallery. There spectators are viewing the art, when one speaks up, "Look at that stupid fellow. He's selfishly indulging his senses while blind to his circumstances. The story then returns to the Zen master. Another tiger runs onto the scene, and now there are two tigers above. The Zen master enjoys his apple, and pretty soon he sees vultures circling overhead. The two tigers have fought and killed each other. The mice see the shadow of the birds and flee. Below a herd of deer comes down to drink from the brook, and the tiger below sets off in pursuit of them. In short, what seemed like dire circumstances fixed themselves or were fixed by some power above.

Years ago a young woman came to me for help. To maintain confidentiality, I will invent a name for her. I'll call her Mary. This young woman in her late thirties had a history of self-mutilation and suicidal behavior. She came in for pastoral counseling, and I agreed to see her only if her psychiatrist agreed and was kept fully informed. That issue out of the way, her first appointment was made. My secretary brought me her file, including the pre-process forms I used. As I reviewed the information in the file, I was taken by the fact that one of her prior therapists was a famous psychiatrist. I thought to myself, "And what on earth am I to do if this person couldn't help her?"

During her first session, the terms of our arrangement were agreed upon. I would see her for ten weeks, once a week, and my conditions and requirements had to be kept. She agreed, and the session began, or perhaps more appropriately, she began sobbing and wailing. An hour passed, and nothing but tears to show for it. Few words could I understand amidst the sobbing. "Until next week," I said, and we parted.

I thought about her for the entire week and decided to try something totally new, at least for me and for that time (circa 1990). I theorized that all the excessive crying was simply her attention-seeking mechanism combined with true feelings of despair, but to get past that, we had to dispense with the wailing. I took a mirror that had been given me by a cosmetic surgeon friend, and which I had used for years to show, as he did, just how uneven the halves of our faces are (left versus right). Brain hemisphere dominance theories suggest a correspondence, so this was in keeping with my research and work.

When Mary visited in week two, she again began crying. I placed the mirror in front of her, explained as nicely as I could that she had to maintain some composure for me to help, told her to look at herself while she cried, and to let me know when she stopped. I stepped out of the office. Soon she opened the door. As I began to sit down, she started weeping again, so once again I exited. After three or four repetitions that admittedly took more than half of our time together, she stopped the sobbing and began talking. Her story was a sad one about a child who was neglected in favor of a younger sibling who was smarter, prettier, and so forth. Her early relationships with men were equally sad but not out of the realm of what happens to psychologically well-balanced people.

When we were finished speaking for the day, it was clear that Mary had dwelled on all the bad, shared her cookies all too willingly, each time probably exaggerating them, and otherwise remained almost fixated on the worst possible future—in her case, becoming a bag lady in Las Vegas.

I gave Mary her homework, as part of our agreed terms. She was to do one good turn for someone, anyone, every day. She was to record the good deed in her journal at bedtime, just before going to sleep, focus on how the deed made her feel, and imagine how it made the recipient feel. The deed could be anything as simple as holding a door for someone or as emotionally demanding as helping a colleague she didn't like. She was to bring the journal with her each week when she visited me.

The following week we reviewed her journal entries and her thoughts and feeling regarding each. Admittedly, some of her first week's good deeds were pretty weak, but a couple of them provided an opportunity to draw out the difference in how it made Mary feel as well as how she might have felt if she had been the recipient. Her homework for the remaining weeks was simple:two good deeds every day and recorded per the earlier instructions.

Mary's perspective changed. Her focus moved from bad things to good things. It was that simple. There is nothing more eloquent than just saying it how it is. Armed with a positive outlook and an eye to opportunities to do good deeds, and supported with what I call a "warm fuzzy feeling" that comes from helping others, Mary began to reinforce her own worth and find joy in living. It wasn't long before her medication was cut back and then eliminated. Mary found meaning in life.

The "warm fuzzy feeling" comes from helping others.

I suggest to you that the real meaning in life comes from what you give, not from what you take. As Wayne Dyer puts it in his book *The*

Power of Intention, purpose is not about vocation—it's about service! I believe that the "warm fuzzy feeling" we derive from a true service experience—going to the aid of another in need—is the best feeling we can have when we put our head on the pillow each night. Gerald Jampolsky has observed in his attitudinal healing centers that when a person goes to the aid of another, even otherwise intractable pain disappears.[15]

The real meaning in life comes from what you give, not from what you take.

I am very fortunate to have many faces in my memories that give to me regularly. There was a time in my life, before the prison study that we'll return to in a moment, that my life was a wreck. Oh, I was successful by most standards—big fancy cars, large homes, rental and recreation property, and so forth, but my personal life was a total wreck. I didn't know how to have a personal relationship unless there was something in it for me. Some of the people around me accused me of changing women as often as most men change shirts. My only life definitions were money and power. From the outside I might have looked like I had something going, but on the inside I was a barren waste. I became agnostic, to say the least, cynical, paranoid, et cetera, and seldom enjoyed a good night's sleep. Fortunately for me, something inside combined with circumstances to show me another choice, an alternative that at the very least held within it peace, balance, harmony, health, and even a sense of purpose.

As another aside, before continuing our prison story, when the centenarian population was studied to determine the reason behind their long lives and health, everyone expected something like "clean living and self-denial." It turned out that that wasn't the case. Indeed, the comedian George Burns could characterize many of the centenarians. They lived life without fear, full of joy and humor. What they all shared was a sense of purpose or connectedness to a Higher Power. The value to this sense of connectedness and purpose cannot be overstated. For me the warm fuzzy feeling keeps me connected and provides purpose. It doesn't really matter what we do for a living, provided we do it with integrity and for the good of others. A piece of Chinese antiquity I cherish is a book written on jade. The author, Su Dong-Puo, a very famous Chinese writer, says it this way: "We do not work or search for food but for truth." As President Woodrow Wilson stated over a thousand years later:

> **"You are not here merely to make a living.**
> **You are here in order to enable the world**
> **to live more amply, with greater vision,**
> **with a finer spirit of hope and achievement.**
> **You are here to enrich the world, and you**
> **impoverish yourself if you forget the errand."**

Back to the inmate population at the Utah State Prison. To undo the blame to produce self-responsible and therefore self-empowered persons, and to move away from the anger-fear loop, I decided on three messages that to this day we include on every InnerTalk program we publish. The three messages:

I forgive myself. I forgive all others. I am forgiven.

We also included statements in first person ("I," not "you," phrases), because subliminal information is processed from the inside out and becomes our words in our stream of consciousness, affirmations designed to build self-esteem and gratitude. At that time, mid-1980, the idea of forgiveness having a therapeutic value was new. Since then many studies, journals, and books have been written about the power of forgiveness.

Okay, what happened with our inmate population? The program worked. The results impressed everyone. The magic bullet, forgiving, together with general affirmations of well-being, worked. The post-test indicated a meaningful result. (If you are interested in more detail, see my book *Subliminal Communication.*) The Utah State Prison officials were as pleased as I, and they followed up by installing libraries of our InnerTalk programs in all of their facilities. When they wanted a program for, say, weight lifting, we did it. Not so the inmate would become stronger per se, but because every single program included the forgiveness messages together with self-esteem units. Other prisons copied the system, and to this day many inmates work with the technology. And me? I went on to a new career.

In conclusion, when you forgive, you essentially undo the ability to blame. If there is nothing to blame, then you are in charge of your response to outside stimuli. There is less room for anger without blame. There is less to fear when you're empowered. The purely pragmatic point is that it works!

In the next chapter, we will take a more thorough look at subliminal information processing and some of the disinformation out there regarding it. Still, if you never use anything else from this book other than the forgiveness lesson, your life will change for the better—and that is a promise! For what it is worth, I want you to know that I had my own epiphanies along the way. I started out trying to fix people, such as the inmates. I soon learned something that Gerald Jampolsky says in his wonderful book *Teach Only Love.* That is this: We teach what we want to learn. I learned the value of life over time, not all at once; the purpose called service, and how to fix myself, not that there still isn't room for improving. In fact, one day I decided that if forgiveness was so important, then our top-selling title at the time, *Forgiving and Letting Go,* should be free. It is free to this day, and you can go to **www.choicesandillusions.com** and get your copy today.

*** ***

A "No" uttered from the deepest conviction is
better and greater than a "Yes" merely uttered
to please, or what is worse, to avoid trouble.

— Mahatma Gandhi

CHAPTER SEVEN

The Nature of a Controversy

When I began my research at the University of Utah library, there was little controversy surrounding the idea of subliminal communication. Early research suggested that this information might even be prioritized by the mind above normally processed verbal information. Since then, this idea has been repeatedly demonstrated, particularly by cognitive psychologists using implicit/explicit memory studies. In this research words are paired, and subjects study the pairing. For example, the word *house* is paired with *chair, green* with *tree,* and so forth. One set of subjects reviews the words with full conscious awareness and attention, seeing the word *chair* followed by the word *house,* while another group receives the word match subliminally, so the word *chair* is seen but the word *house* is presented subliminally. These studies repeatedly demonstrate higher matches for the group that receives the subliminal match word.

The advantage to subliminal affirmations is obvious. I often demonstrate this in seminars by asking the participants, *Who would like to make a million dollars this year?* All hands go up. Then I instruct the audience to say to themselves with meaning, "I'm going to make a million dollars this year!" Within just a few seconds smiles begin to shine from faces in the audience as they get back their true inner belief: "Sure, what are you going to do, rob a bank?" The fact is that to make a million dollars, we must believe we can. If Bill Gates were in the audience, his goal would not be one million dollars because that is far too little for him. No, his expectation and true inner belief would put a much higher number in place.

I am going to make a million dollars this year.

Telling ourselves we can or will do something, such as losing weight, has value, but that value is mitigated by our own true inner belief. Our inner belief must change for change to occur. When subliminal information is processed, it enters our stream of consciousness. It literally becomes our own self-talk. In time it simply overwhelms a lot of the no/don't, I can't, and other information that is our chicken yard learning. Soon we believe the message "I am good" instead of challenging it with such statements as "Good at what? Do you remember when?"

However, the field of subliminal information processing was becoming controversial. At the height of the controversy, the famous civil lawsuit involving Judas Priest was tried. I was asked to look at the information by the plaintiff's attorneys, who had brought a wrongful death action against CBS (the publisher) and Judas Priest. I had testified as a so-called expert witness before but that did not prepare me for some of what followed my deposition and testimony in this case. There was definitely an orchestrated campaign to discredit witnesses and testimony that might argue subliminal information is not only perceived but also acted upon. In my instance, the press had some real fun. For example, I had friends phone and ask if I had seen the Joan Rivers show on CBS? I had not seen the show, so they informed me that I had been portrayed as a mail-order minister who was a high-school dropout. "Truth," I used to say when conducting lie-detection interviews, "knows no percentages. It is either complete or omitting. A substantial relevant omission is deception. No one wants their significant other to be 99 percent faithful. Truth is either 100 percent or it's not the truth."

The truth to the Joan River's statements may be literally correct, I still have not seen the show, but they are out of context and substantially omitting relevant information. As a senior in high school in my last semester and holding a perfect 4.0 (A) GPA, I was called into Reed Call's office, the principal of Granger High School. He informed me that since I had missed several days of school (I lived on my own and held at least one job while attending school to pay for board, room, clothing and so forth) and since the school was reimbursed $1.00 a day for attendance, they could not graduate me. I would have to make up the lost dollars to the school by attending summer school. There was a month or so of high school left, and I had been informed of a postgraduate scholarship if I graduated on schedule. As a hot-headed young 18-year-old, I basically told Mr. Call, who I must admit I had no respect for based on other incidents, to put his diploma where the proverbial sun doesn't shine. I left the high school and never went back.

At the age of twenty-five, I decided to return to school. I matriculated at Weber State College in Ogden, Utah. No high school equivalency such as the GED was required based on my admission test scores. Indeed, my scores on the College Level Examination for Proficiency (CLEP) provided a year's worth of college credit. At the time, I thought I wanted to go to law school, so after three years at Weber, I applied to McGeorge College of Law and they had me take a college-equivalency examination at the University of Pacific that again I passed. Things in my life changed about then, so I did not go to law school. The long and the short of it comes down to this. I invested thousands of dollars and hours in alternative distance education as well as week-long intensives. Along the way I earned a doctorate in psychology, became a Diplomate in the American Psychotherapy Association and so forth, and of course an ordained minister. My ministerial schooling at the University of Metaphysics (**www.metaphysics.com**) was among the best time and money I invested. It was a correspondence program conducted in a distance learning format, so I suppose it is somewhat true, I am a mail-order minister who dropped out of high school.

However, back to the Judas Priest trial. The case involved two young men who, after drinking a few beers while repeatedly playing the song "Better by You, Better Than Me," from the *Stained Class* album by Judas Priest, took a shotgun to the playground and shot themselves (this account is also provided in my book *Thinking Without Thinking*).

Two teenage boys had difficulty adjusting to life. Ray had just split up with his girlfriend. James had just lost his job. Neither of them was blameless. Both of them were confused. For most young people, the approach to adulthood provides struggles. It should.

Two days before Christmas, Ray gave James a gift of music. The music had particular significance. James had once collected the music of this particular artist, but when he found the music violated his Christian beliefs, he threw it all away.

That was a few years before. James no longer pursued any religious affiliation. He had turned away from religion. Many people do at some point in their lives.

On December 23rd, James received the album. The boys decided to play the album while they drank beer. The words and music of one song held their interest. They played it repeatedly. The lyrics in several songs encouraged suicide with such rhymes as "Leave this life with all its sin / It's not fit for living in."

Picture these two young men, attractive, on the slight side—skinny, according to more than one description—unskilled, not doing well in school, anticipating a life of difficulty and with delusions of grandeur driven by frustration, pretending to be mercenaries, or imagining themselves as heroes.

By mid-afternoon, the lyrics going around in their heads included, "Why do you have to die to be a hero?" The two looked at each other as though acting in some movie. The hero says, "Let's do it!" just before mayhem begins. One of the boys said, "Do it!" The two began chanting, "Do it." One of them grabbed a shotgun. They went out the bedroom window to the church playground. Ray placed a shotgun under his jaw. James chanted, "Do it!" Ray fired the gun. The blast stunned James. Ray was dead.

James lifted the gun, wet with blood. He said later that he trembled. He felt afraid. He could be blamed for Ray's death. He wondered why they had chanted, "Do it." He placed the gun under his own jaw. He pulled the trigger.

But James had failed to brace the shotgun. As he pulled the trigger, the gun lurched forward. The blast shot off the front of his face. It did not kill him. It left him severely wounded and disfigured. He lived for nearly three years.

After reviewing the case, I took the position, unpopular as it turned out to be, that the subliminal command "Do it!" was a causal factor in the double shooting. The point we are interested in here is not the details of the case, although you can find them in my book, *Thinking Without Thinking*. Rather, it is the birth of a scientific controversy. Prior to this case, Congressional hearings in 1984 had led to the most significant source of scientific controversy, which was simply whether or not a subliminal message could affect behavior. Lloyd Silverman said yes, and Howard Shevrin was doubtful.[16] In the Judas Priest case, Shevrin switched positions based on newer research and agreed with me: The subliminal "Do it" command was a causal factor.[17]

You might wonder, so what was the controversy? A new study conducted by a marketing student on the influence of labels was being announced everywhere—and I do mean everywhere, from *Seventeen* magazine to prime time news. This study purportedly proved that subliminal messages did not work to influence behavior. (Again, you can read all the details of this study and the Congressional hearings in my book.)

A psychologist I have great respect for supervised the study. Unfortunately, the study itself did not achieve what the media or the pundits who sided with CBS claimed it did. So you understand why I say that, let me go through the study in some detail.

By design, the study evaluated the influence of labels on the consumer. To do this, the doctoral student who set up the research project sought and obtained subliminal audiotapes from five different companies. The tapes were of two kinds, one to improve memory and one to build esteem. The labels on the tapes were then changed so that the esteem tapes were labeled memory and vice versa. The pretest instruments measured memory and esteem. After the test period, subjects were brought back and tested for actual improvement. Subjects who thought they were playing memory subliminal messages reported an improvement in memory and subjects who believed they were listening to esteem messages reported an increase in their esteem. The instruments failed to identify a statistically meaningful change in either. Fair enough, at this point, to state a definite label influence, but how about a real effect regarding subliminal communication?

The five tape companies all claimed different methods and messages for their programs, including messages in the second person and messages in the first person. Audio analysis failed to recover messages on any of the programs. (Remember my Audio Forensic Labs test?) According to an affidavit from the sound engineer, at least one major manufacturer of audio subliminal programs mixed messages 40 db beneath the carrier (music or ocean sounds). This 40 db is beneath the theoretical limit of most players. In other words, the signal strength might be compared to the influence of a whisper two blocks away. It might be that the messages were not recoverable because the *secret* method used included such a mixing procedure. Other companies used questionable affirmations and in other ways produced material that differentiated one company from another. All shared the label "subliminal," but that certainly did not mean they were the "same."

Let me give you an example to clarify the importance of this difference. Assume a scientist pressurizes a trapped atmosphere to, say, ten atmospheric pressures, applies an exact electric charge, and then heats the result. To replicate this study, a researcher would determine the nature of the atmosphere that was trapped and replicate the process, including the exact degree of heat and electric current applied. Now assume that someone attempts to replicate the study by catching room atmosphere in a fish bowl and covering it with plastic wrap so it is trapped. He places a nine-volt battery inside the fish bowl and then heats it with a cigarette lighter. Hardly the same experiment. Let's now take it a step further. Imagine that five fish bowl makers all use different elements but claim the same outcome. Is testing all five bowl makers the same as replicating the original study? The answer is clear: NO! Even if one of the bowl makers has it right, the other four would contaminate the outcome.

So, we are not looking at a scientific study with a single variable. We are mixing multiple variables and coming up with a single conclusion—and that simply is not good science! Nevertheless, this study was in the media everywhere, and those testifying for CBS and Judas Priest were touting it almost as if it were the Holy Grail.

The long and the short of this case comes down to a few facts. Judas Priest admitted to putting subliminal content on some recordings but not this one. When the messages were demonstrated to be present, the counter argument was it occurred only as a "coincidence of sound." CBS was fined more than once by the judge for impeding the discovery process and manipulating the press. It was CBS Records' own disclosure of the boys chanting, "Do it." CBS's own investigator, a former Scotland Yard detective, stated that he was unable to locate the original 24-track master and that he was never allowed to look in the CBS vault. (The original master was needed in order to prove the message was not a coincidence of sound). In a wrongful death action, intent must be demonstrated. This was not a product liability suit, as would be the case with defective brakes on an automobile.

The evidence for influence of behavior due to subliminal messages has even been admitted by some of the most outspoken persons.

The result of the press attention and managed or manipulated media gave rise to the real scientific controversy. Since then, the power of subliminal messages to influence behavior has been admitted by some of the most outspoken persons defending the position of CBS.

Even the *Skeptical Enquirer,* a science journal that has a history of debunking many things later proven to be true, admits evidence for behavior changes due to subliminal stimuli,[18] and they published a number of scientific articles supposedly debunking the subliminal influence during and following the Judas Priest trial. The definitive work of Robert Bornstein and his meta-analysis approach shows clearly that a properly delivered (signal strength) psychoactive message (affirmation) can and does influence behavior.[19] The fact of the matter is, as Bornstein put it to me in a telephone conversation following a television filming for the Discovery channel, the effects of subliminal stimuli on humans, including behavior, is so robust in the literature that you have got to wonder where individuals who deny it have been in the last ten years.

The research on InnerTalk includes over a dozen double-blind studies conducted by independent researchers at leading institutions throughout the world and on a number of domains ranging from Attention Deficit Hyperactive Disorder to depression (see Appendix A for more information). The model is simple and was first put forward by Albert Ellis.[20]

The A-B-C model, as it is called, is graphically depicted as follows:

A————————————> B————————————> C
(activating event)　　(belief)　　　(consequence:
　　　　　　　　　　　　　　　　　　emotional and behavioral)

An activating event, stimulus, or verbal affirmation, affects belief, which equals emotional and behavioral consequences. It is easy to see this rather linear in-and-out when looking at the negative input in our lives, and it works more or less in the same way with respect to the positive. Ellis coined a term for negative self-talk that is best known as ANTS—Automatic Negative Thoughts. I like this term because it is easy to imagine ants tearing down your positive thoughts and carrying in the negative. Perhaps the next time the ants are bugging you, you can do what I do. Just imagine a little ant bait and let them feed. You can simply follow a negative thought with something like "And then what?" Eventually the "then whats" lose their power. Even a "then you die" is not threatening when you remember you are a creation of the Divine—but back to our story.

During the Judas Priest trial I was asked if I had ever conducted a research design that indicated a person would kill himself as a result of a subliminal message. "Of course not" had to be my answer. No scientist I know of would even consider doing such a thing, at least I hope not. Then an idea came to me. What if a person received a subliminal message of danger?

A pilot study was arranged. My daughter, Hillarie, who was working on a science project for high school, accepted my suggestion and obtained the appropriate guidance and permissions from all involved.

Group A listened to the sounds of ocean with three subliminal information deliveries, approximately one minute apart. The messages were "DANGER, DANGER, WATCH OUT!—AH-H-H-G-H! DANGER!" The messages were recorded and delivered simultaneously in both forward and reversed speech. Group B listened to the same ocean track with the message "People are walking."

Both groups listened to the tapes for four minutes, with earphones, while their body responses were monitored for changes in breathing, blood pressure, the electrical resistance of their skin, and the moisture at the end of their fingers. A four-needle polygraph, the same instrument used as a "lie detector," recorded these responses.

After the four-minute trial each subject responded to a questionnaire that included a request to report any particular reverie, feelings or thoughts that occurred during the trials. Only then did an assistant discover and reveal to the subject which group he or she was in.

All five of those in group A responded with gross reactions or changes in the measurements of body function coinciding with the delivery of the subliminal "danger" message. Those in the B group had no such response. This suggests a danger-stimulus recognition. The bodies of the subjects in group A responded as though an actual danger existed. So did their minds. Three of the five in group A reported reveries of killing or being killed. A fourth person reported feeling extremely upset. The fifth said she was too occupied by what the experimenters were doing to notice her thoughts. (The experimenters were doing very little.) Psychological theory has categories of fantasy formation. Our response to danger, the fight/flight response, can generate compelling fantasies.

When a person feels threatened, fight/flight gives rise to thoughts of this nature. Killing is fight oriented, and death may be flight oriented. Many deal with fear, in fantasy, by neutralizing the source of the fear—even if it means killing. Dying, on the other hand, means escape to many. Of five normal, healthy teenagers, four had thoughts of killing or dying. The fifth apparently "blanked out." This came from one listening, in a pleasant and sober state, to a few repetitions of a single, simple, subliminal message for a few minutes.

Those who heard the message "People are walking" had reveries that went like this: "I was at a sunny beach, and there were a lot of people."

I have since posted this study together with all needed materials, including downloadable sound files, as an academic challenge at **www.progressiveawareness.org**. No one has run the study with a different outcome.

Today, the science of subliminals is still hyped and poorly understood by many, but it is a true science with valid merits. It truly can assist in enabling individuals to overcome their doubts and fears and negative input that all too often create self-imposed limitations.

It is not uncommon for musical groups to use subliminal information, as I suggested earlier. In 1991 I was contacted by WNCI radio regarding satanic messages in a Madonna recording. Not only were the messages there, but also her people later admitted to putting them there for publicity purposes. Here are some of those messages delivered in poetic format:

In the midnight smoke of yellow
Hear my melodies
Hail to the family
It must be unknown
Hail hallelujah my position . . .

The influence media has over our thoughts and actions is worth spending just another moment on. For years I have had a proverbial pet peeve against the selling of illness. For example, every year we are told through the media, chiefly television, that the dreaded "gomboo" is coming to town. We are also told we'll probably catch it, as if we were going to run down the street and catch a cold (notice those words, please). But that's okay, because there is a remedy, and when we take it we will be pampered in bed like the characters acting out the TV commercial.

We all are exposed to fancy cars with beautiful people paired with them, as if when we want something beautiful in our lives, or to be sexy and so forth, we need this product to obtain it. Most of us are aware of this kind of advertising, and still it can influence us.

There are general categories applied to the definition of subliminal communication through any media. Wolman sets out the categories this way:[21]

WOLMAN'S CATEGORIES

Professor Benjamin B. Wolman's modified categorization of subliminal stimuli divides descriptive values into four criteria of awareness and unawareness. The stimuli are as follows:

1. Below the level of registration.
2. Above the level of registration but below the level of detection.
3. Above the level of detection and discrimination but below the level of identification.*
4. Below the level of identification only because of a defensive action.

Using Wolman's categories, our patented InnerTalk technology falls into category three.

Wolman, B.B. (1973)

Embeds such as those in the liquor advertisement discussed earlier may well fit into category 4. Messages such as those in Madonna and Judas Priest generally fit into category 3. A category 2 subliminal message may well be the type flashed on a screen, such as the reported popcorn and cola flashes in the infamous New Jersey theater instance. A category 1 is the message mixed at 40 db beneath the music when played on a stereo with a db limitation of 30.

In the next chapter we will look at the nature of the mind and other influences that contribute to the makeup of the total human condition, including the so-called paranormal.

*** ***

All I have seen teaches me to trust the Creator
for all I have not seen.
— Ralph Waldo Emerson

CHAPTER EIGHT

Mind Is Not a Local Event

Mind. Consciousness. What is it we mean when we use these words? Dr. Bruce Lipton once told me of an experiment that I shared in my book *Wellness: Just a State of Mind?* Dividing cells scraped with a tongue depressor, half remained in a petri dish in the laboratory and the other half were taken five miles away. On cue, the cells in the lab were shocked with low voltage current. The cells five miles away immediately responded as if they were in the dish back in the lab. Cell consciousness? Indeed, according to Lipton's book *The Biology of Belief,* not only are the cells conscious, but they also respond to thoughts and beliefs—and the 'they' in cells includes the DNA. The DNA can be "turned on" by belief, or, in the words of Dr. Ernest Lawrence Rossi, "The mind drives the body, which drives the genetic code." The implications lead Rossi to this conclusion: "The dynamics of gene expression and brain plasticity can be initiated within the time frame of a typical psychotherapy session."

"The mind drives the body, which drives the genome."

Cleve Baxter became famous overnight, not for his lie-detection school or his special version of the polygraph, but for his plants. Headlines ran: "Your Plants May Tell on You." Cleve wired a philodendron to the GSR readings of a polygraph. Three subjects passed through the room, looking first at the goldfish in the bowl next to the plant, then at a Bunsen burner heating water, and then at the plant. The same three passed through a second time, but this time the last one took a goldfish and dropped it in boiling water. The plant responded as though it were conscious, aware and even shocked at what happened.

Then, in a stroke of genius, Cleve mixed up the order in which the subjects entered the room. Every time the fish cooker entered the room, the plant responded. The plant was apparently identifying the perpetrator, perhaps in fear. What do you think?

There is a tremendous new interest in the study of consciousness. For years the subject was taboo in science simply because it was seen as inherently unverifiable. That is, your consciousness and my consciousness are uniquely subjective. Science is all about objective and verifiable inquiry. Indeed, the scientific method requires that. Today, in part due to investigations directed at artificial intelligence and new experimental designs, consciousness is again being examined.

What is consciousness? Language is often thought to be the tool of consciousness and evidence for the kind of consciousness that makes humans different from monkeys. Indeed, language has often been referred to as the "jewel of cognition." Some scientists have argued that Neanderthal man possessed advanced talking ability. This assertion is largely based upon a neck bone found in 1988.[22] Other scientists argue for a more recent origin to speech—recent in this sense being between 50 and 100 thousand years ago. By contrast, early origin theorists date the beginning of language at more than 2 million years ago.

What is consciousness?

The evolution and history of language have a bearing on certain philosophical issues where consciousness is concerned. For example, take any date for the first appearance of language. For fun, let's just assume some hairy bipedal creature that has never spoken. Is this creature conscious? Conscious in the sense humans are conscious? Now one day the creature utters some meaningful form of speech. Not a grunt or guttural sound, as all animals do, but some form— beginning—of speech. Is the creature now conscious?

What is the difference between the consciousness of animals and the consciousness of humans? What is intended by distinguishing between the two conscious forms as different and why? If a primate species shows the ability to learn, remember, and associate learnings, some insist this is evidence for reason. Most flatly refuse to recognize it as such. Is it possible that by recognizing consciousness as worthy and ripe for study that man's consciousness will lose its unique, elevated status? What precisely is it that one means by consciousness, anyway?

Certainly reason preceded language. It would be rather odd if it were the other way around. Still, that's an interesting thought.

Some seem to reason only with the tools of their language. In other words, their reason is limited by the rules and definitions of their language. Plus, there is some argument in favor of certain language structure as having greater or lesser faculties for developing logical thinking. Literal languages such as German, for example, tend to encourage the development of logical thinkers. However intriguing this may be, it still seems reasonable that reason preceded the conceptualization and development of speech. As such, one is hard pressed to limit the consciousness of a species on the basis of sound patterns called speech.

It gets still tougher. Sound patterns that resemble speech are uttered by so-called nonconscious animals such as whales and dolphins. So, what is consciousness?

Is consciousness a matter of wakefulness? No, it can't be just that, for one can be a conscious being and still be asleep. Is consciousness memory? According to the experiments of Cleve Baxter, plants exhibit memory. Since science abandoned the study of consciousness years ago, the problems inherent in describing consciousness have proliferated during the interim. The advent of animal studies, plant studies, and synthetic or artificial intelligence has greatly complicated the matters of consciousness. Or perhaps simplified them.

For most people, parts of the left brain handle language. Brain hemispheric studies, including the now popular Positron Emission Tomography (PET) scans show that the right ear sends acoustic information to the left hemisphere. According to Marc Hauser of Harvard University and Karin Andersson of Radcliff College in Cambridge, rhesus monkeys "display a similar cerebral setup, with the left half of the brain often taking responsibility for vocalizations intended to signal aggression."[23] If that is true, does it mean that the anatomical evidence for language processing is evidence for consciousness in the sense that we normally think of mankind's consciousness. If not, what are the differences?

For some, *mind* equals *brain*. But for many, *mind* is a more general term that refers to the processes handled by the brain. Therefore, *mind* is often used interchangeably with *consciousness*. Is *mind* equal to *brain?* The chief area of inquiry offering evidence one way or another to answer this question is a discipline often held in low regard. Still, literally thousands of laboratory experiments in scientific parapsychology demonstrate that many aspects of mind cannot be reduced to anatomical or material brain.

For example, data clearly supports the "reality" of telepathy, clairvoyance, and psychokinesis. Indeed, although controversial, recent Russian DNA research explains much of this phenomena (clairvoyance, intuition, spontaneous healing, etc) and proposes that DNA can be influenced by words and frequencies, not unlike the claim of Rossi.[24] Joining linguists and geneticists, the Russian scientists claim to have found that the alkalines in the so-called useless 90 percent "junk DNA" follows rules similar to those of all languages. Further, according to Pjotr Garjajev, "living chromosomes function just like a holographic computer using endogenous DNA laser radiation."[25] This simply means that as McTaggart reported in her book *The Field*, vibrating the DNA at a particular frequency could theoretically influence the DNA information itself.[26]

The biographies of some of the world's most respected people provide a richer picture than can be found even in science. Famous people throughout history have provided rich reports of their experiences with the so-called paranormal. Throughout the world and even in America's capital, Washington, D.C., there exist numerous paranormal reports, ranging from Abraham Lincoln's ghost wandering the White House to the Reagan Administration's use of psychics. The point is simple. Whether it is from the genius of Einstein or the laboratory of a modern parapsychologist, mind is not equal to brain! What does that mean with respect to consciousness?

A wonderful *Star Trek* adventure I can remember had the *Enterprise* actually forming its own consciousness and then creating a new life form. Somehow, as Mr. Data explained, the activity of the starship's computers and records began to take on a "more than the sum of the parts" activity, form its own neural network, and so forth. Will machines ever become conscious?

This was the headline in a *Science News* publication: "Simulated Creatures Evolve and Learn." The article, by Richard Lipkin, cited the work of Karl Sims of *Thinking Machines* in Cambridge, Mass., who "devised a simulated evolutionary system in which virtual creatures compete for resources in a three-dimensional arena. . . . The creatures, resembling toy-block robots, enter one-on-one contests in which they vie for control of a desired object—an extra cube. Winners—deemed fit—reproduce, while losers bear no offspring. Sims endows the virtual environment with physical parameters, such as gravity and friction, and restricts behaviors to plausible physical actions."[27] Sims believes that it may be easier to evolve virtual entities with intelligent behavior than to create them from scratch. Artificial-intelligence researchers have long sought to develop the so-called thinking machine. Unlike Sims, most begin by attempting to model the computer after the patterns of man. For some, this is the neural model of the brain while for others it is the deductive/inductive model of reason. Perhaps Sims' method is more manlike than the other two. Mankind is thought to have evolved. Does this help us understand consciousness? What about the collective of consciousness? Will machines soon be contributing to this field of consciousness? Will a machine ever dream?

The "Genius Hypothesis," advanced by Ervin Laszlo,[28] asserts that the minds "of unusually creative people are in spontaneous, direct, though usually not conscious, interaction with other minds in the creative process itself." Laszlo's paper sheds light on the "archetypal experience" described by Carl Jung while using history, physics, psychology, artistic production, and cultural development to clearly suggest the strong possibility (in my opinion, the only real possibility) that not only do minds communicate but they do so at a distance as well!

Not only do minds communicate, but they do so at a distance as well!

Is the collective, or the shared, consciousness experience an independent consciousness? Is it possible that unique (individual) conscious entities participate as transceivers, sending and receiving, and that the total of consciousness is this collective? Does the collective have a plan, a will? Does it dream? Or is it just a repository? Does it have a neural network or some analogous something that we might refer to as a nonspatial field? It's not organic or silicone, is it?

Perhaps consciousness is something that has to do with being conscious of consciousness. Are monkeys truly conscious of being conscious? Could they even entertain the idea of consciousness without an object? Or consciousness as a character in someone else's dream? Does a monkey ask itself if it really exists?

Is that a fair direction to take our questions regarding consciousness? After all, are we not likely to be forced to admit the notion of "devolution" if we do? Are there not altogether too many *homo sapien sapiens* on the planet that don't give the proverbial "hoot" about who they are or where they came from? How many of these people ask the question, "Do I really exist?" Will silicone ask the question, "Who am I?" The Japanese have already built a "Darwin machine." The artificial brain uses an evolving neural network. Hugo de Garis says the purpose is to produce a silicone brain with more than one billion artificial neurons.

Science News says this machine "will come in the form of a neural network and will exist within a massively parallel computer. To create such a complex system, the researchers will have the network build itself. 'Cellular automata,' each one a distinct computer program, will actually forge their own linkages."

This approach, called "evolutionary engineering," provides for the growth of the silicone brain via connections. "The neural net grows when cellular automata send 'growth signals' to each other, then connect via synapses."[29] (And you thought genetic engineering was something to wonder about.)

Defining consciousness turns out to be a process somewhat akin to searching for the core of an onion. Revisiting consciousness is more than a philosophical exercise or a scientific inquiry. It is a duty, even a moral imperative, to reevaluate the nature of consciousness, for this inherently devises the strategy by which mankind treats itself and all life. For me, and I suspect for many others, many changes are necessary for the human race to actualize the highest of its potentials. As in history, most certainly some of these changes will be brought about by difficult times. I am reminded of something Martin Luther King said: "I can never be what I ought to be, until you are what you ought to be." King pointed out that it is precisely the interrelated fabric of life that each of us is interdependent upon.

> **"I can never be what I ought to be,**
> **until you are what you ought to be."**
> — Martin Luther King

Perhaps it is the interrelated nature of all life, consciousness itself, upon which we are interdependent. Perhaps, just perhaps, mankind will only know his highest, most noble self when he offers the deepest respect for all life. Perhaps the invigorated enthusiasm searching for a firm hold on this stuff called consciousness will eventually give rise to the respect I speak of. Perhaps the Zero Point nature of consciousness now being experimented with by respectable physicists will yield access, conscious access, to the One Mind of the Universe. (This concept is especially interesting but also somewhat technical. For a great review of the work, see Lynne McTaggart's book *The Field: The Quest for the Secret Force of the Universe*.)

Is it possible that our minds are indeed some sort of sophisticated transceiver?

Rupert Sheldrake has demonstrated what he calls the M Field. People who are taught Morse Code in a dedicated room experience both an easier learning curve and greater retention after previous groups have studied Morse Code in the same room.[30] Is it possible that our minds are indeed some sort of sophisticated transceiver? If so, is tuning into love and light versus greed, avarice, and anger just a matter of the station we choose to listen to?

Meditation studies have shown that when groups meditate on peace, crime rates fall.[31] New research into life after death, particularly the work by Dr. Gary Schwartz (see his book *The Afterlife Experiments*) that employed ever more rigorous designs, has yielded surprising evidence for life after death.[32] Near-death experiences have not been adequately explained by the so-called debunkers, and the data suggesting parapsychological abilities just keep increasing.

In my lifetime many of my associates and acquaintances have challenged the paranormal. Many scientists and sciolistic thinkers often treat this subject as totally foolish and unscientific. The so-called paranormal or psychic phenomena, the near-death experiences, the reports of reincarnation, astral projection, auras, and so forth are all dumped into a bin of laughable irrelevance reported by delusional people or individuals under the influence of chemistry, including their own brain chemistry, such as is argued with near-death experiences.

Not all scientists view the extraordinary with such disdain and ignorance, however. Indeed, some of the greatest thinkers of all time, including this century, have conducted solid research and otherwise made serious scientific inquiries that have led to conclusions favoring a nonlocal mind interacting in a holographic universe via principles of mind, including thought and belief, and thereby co-creating what most call reality. It is definitely worth noting that as Lynne McTaggart points out in her book *The Intention Experiment*, science has clearly demonstrated that "thought is a tangible thing with the power to affect the physical world!"[33] In a private communication with me, Ms. McTaggart added this: "We've played around with the idea for many hundreds of years that our thoughts can change the world around us. For most, though, it's an idea that has been dismissed as so much wishful thinking. But dig a little deeper—as I have been doing—and you discover extraordinary evidence to suggest that this really is possible, that out thoughts are another form of energy that impacts and influences the so-called physical. So now we're taking this a step further, and we're carrying out a series of experiments and incorporating the new InnerTalk CD produced just for this experiment. This will be the largest global study ever undertaken." The Intention Experiment will be supervised by several notable scientists and is designed to demonstrate that human's intentions can actually change the world around them. If you would like to participate, visit her web site at **www.intentionexperiment.com**.

Great books have been written in just the past decade that reveal a universe quite different from the one taught in high school physics. Charles Harper's work *Spiritual Information,* Lynne McTaggart's *The Field,* Fritjof Capra's book *The Web of Life,* Michael Talbot's work *The Holographic Universe,* Amit Goswami's eloquent book *Physics of the Soul,* and so many more clearly convolute the expectation of most with a new world view that has mind inextricably connected with what we think of as matter and reality. I do not wish to slight any of the writers and scientists who are contributing to this remarkable revolution in physics, so please accept that the works cited above are but a few of the great ones now in print. (A recommended list of readings is in the back of the book.) Suffice it to say, consciousness, mind, or whatever you wish to call the quintessential you, is not local, not body, not ego, not what you might have believed in the past, but much greater than we can imagine. In a very real sense, the quintessential you is, in the words of Plotinus, "ineffable." The bottom line is this: Phenomena and miracles happen!

For my part, I have always known as much. As a small boy I had experiences that cannot be explained other than by some paranormal means. I somehow noetically knew things without knowing how I knew. I was able to locate lost objects, identify disturbances around people, and so forth. In fact, I have found in my years of traveling and lecturing that most young people have similar experiences but learn to shut them down because of the ridicule that comes in the name of "imagination." It's all in your imagination, as if imagination were itself a bad thing.

As a teenager, I experienced something that I can never forget. Let me share that story with you, for part of making your choice about whatever life you wish to have is influenced by your view of this world and any possible afterlife.

One evening with my date, a beautiful young woman named Connie Bennet, I set out to pick up some money due me before going to a dance. We were driving in a 1957 Oldsmobile, and on the outskirts of the small town of Woods Cross I began to tease Connie that we were running out of gas. It was very dark, and I stepped on the gas and then let off quickly, thereby causing the car to jerk and lunge. We were approaching several sets of railroad tracks, and as we climbed up onto one, the car engine died. As if on cue, signal arms descended and lights began to flash. To my left I could see the headlight of the train engine bearing down on us. It seemed to be coming very fast so when Connie asked if we should get out of the car, the only thing I could think of was Connie stumbling and the car being dragged over her, so I said, "No, let me try and start the car." I turned the key, realizing the engine was flooded, and held the gas to the floor while I did so, for the 1957 Oldsmobile we were in had a Carter carburetor and when it was flooded, the gas pedal was to be down while the engine was started.

Connie had her hand on my leg while I frantically tried to start the engine. The next thing I knew, though, was not Connie asking for me, because I was not in the car. To be absolutely clear, I *was* in the car when the train smashed into us and *not* there when Connie was being freed.

As Connie was cut from the wreckage, and this took some time, she asked about me. The driver's side of the automobile had been crushed under the cattle guard before the car was spun and dragged down the tracks. As a result, the driver's side was only three feet high or so. As it turned out, the train consisted of approximately 100 cars and was traveling at about 100 miles per hour. I know this because of the ensuing court case, for Connie was injured and for years wore a neck brace.

The first thing I knew after the train hit us was that I was standing alone in a field alongside the railroad tracks, perhaps fifty yards from many emergency vehicles, all with their lights flashing. Several automobiles were backed up behind the now-stopped train. Some time had clearly elapsed because Connie was not still being extracted from the car. No, she was in an ambulance, about to leave for the hospital. My first thoughts were about her, so I ran to the emergency vehicles, where I was questioned. I was taken to Connie as soon as those in charge learned that I had been driving the car.

What I have just shared with you is not possible—but it happened. My mother suggested a few weeks later that perhaps I was a walk-in, insisting that I had changed. (A walk-in is thought by some to occur when a spirit of a being chooses to leave and another spirit steps in). I didn't even know, at that time, what a walk-in was; what I did know was guilt for Connie's suffering. I tried to shut out the whole experience and to some extent was quite successful for many years. However, the universe had different plans for me, and one day decided to bring it all back.

Mind is not a local event.

My point here is simple: Mind is not a local event. Whatever mind is, we share it in many ways. Consciousness is not understood, let alone properly defined. The rectorship of life, whatever life is, includes events and experiences that defy normal explanations and thus become paranormal. We are all much more than just a physical body with an organic brain sending signals along neural pathways like some sophisticated piece of machinery. Consciousness connects all of us in some manner or another and it would appear to survive. As I once wrote in *The Little Black Book,* when we die we do not take with us our fancy cars, our houses, our awards and diplomas, and so forth. No, the only thing that survives with us is our relationships.

*** ***

An error doesn't become a mistake
until you refuse to correct it.
— O. A. Battista

CHAPTER NINE

The Subtraction Game

It is a natural human characteristic to desire a certain quality of life. As such, it is fair to ask, *What is quality of life?* Most, when thoughtful, consider quality of life to include at least the following three characteristics: 1. Absence of fear, 2. Loving relationships (support), and 3. Fulfillment of necessities (food, water, shelter, health care, and so forth). Contrasted against the typical self-image, a couple of issues immediately emerge. First among them is the fear generated within ourselves over the risk of exposure or rejection. Next, the distance generated between people when genuine and total honesty is not forthcoming in a relationship. Third is concern over the most basic needs in life due to an absence of self-confidence—confidence in the ability to provide, especially into retirement. The common denominator in all of this is obvious—fear.

What is fear but an emotional assumption that we lack the ability to negotiate a desired quality of life? When cast in the light of Singer's four representations discussed earlier (actual self, ideal self, ought-to-be self, and desired self), where in the mental rehearsals of self does this fear arise? Does it root itself in the actual self, the ideal self, the ought-to-be self, or the desired self—or is it rooted in the differential between them?

The answer, in my opinion, is all of the above. Typically, our mental rehearsals do not include reconciliation of the selves, so to speak. That is, the original childhood rehearsals are perpetuated in some form or another into adulthood. We rehearse what we might have said, or how we should have responded, and these rehearsals are just as glamorous in a "Hollywood" sense of the word as they were when we were children. This glamorous perspective seeks to make heroes or heroines out of us. It is a game the famous philosopher Krishnamurti called "One-Upmanship."[34] All too often, it is a "get-even or get-evener" response that seeks to claim some victory, at least in our minds, that is rehearsed. Like a child, some seem tethered to the notion that their worth is fragile and best redeemed at the expense of others. In other words, if I make someone else feel inferior, then I have established my own superiority.

It is a strange world we live in when the criteria for establishing one's self-worth are based on the subtraction method. Subtract from John and Sally and Luke, and we somehow gain? The mature adult recognizes quickly the fallacy inherent in this kind of thinking. The circular nature of getting even or "getting evener" creates a world of insecurities and distortions, both in the physical and the mental. Robert Laing has stated that the condition of the normal man is one of self-alienation.[35] Laing continues with strong words that are altogether too true, insisting that man pretends to be what he is not until he loses what he is.

The truth is that whenever we denigrate another, we subtract from ourselves. To the precise degree that we make less of another, we make less of ourselves. Further, this precedent subtracts from all of humanity's potential. Mankind's unkind tolerance for unkind deeds perpetuates only unkindness. Thus, fear itself is fed both by the acts of unkindness and by the inherit circularity of getting even.

Here is a Taoist saying: "What we resist we become." In our resistance to being mocked, ridiculed, criticized, or in any other way treated in some undignified way, we create the very thing we desire to eliminate. We choose to "fight fire with fire" and in the end find ourselves burning away our own dignity and potential. All of this begins with our mental rehearsals, most of which arise from scenes right out of some television or theatrical presentation. Hollywood heroes and heroines of the kind portrayed in get-even events may make cute sit-coms but not serious role models.

Remember our flowerpot story? Can you imagine a Hollywood production that portrayed such a thing? Have you ever made such a mental rehearsal? Think about it this way: Of the potential outcomes in the various scenarios, which one is going to make you feel good twenty years later? Which choice is going to feed your character, your esteem, and your integrity in years to come? Which will subtract from your sense of personal well-being?

The box many find themselves in is self-defining and confining.

Thinking out of the box, so to speak, is the kind of thinking all of us must do if we are to get out of the box. The box many find themselves in is self-defining and confining. The walls of the box are fear, anger, lack, and so forth. Some circle the walls, pacing like trapped animals, failing to look up from their feet enough to see just how easy the walls are to step over.

The walls of the box are fear, anger, lack, and so forth.

The longest journey, Lao-tzu stated, begins with a single step. Recognizing the walls for exactly what they are and how they got there is the first step in freeing ourselves. Deciding to step out of the confines of "the same old, same old" is the next step. It is a new, genuine choice. It is a change in beliefs.

Belief is a powerful force. Belief makes a sugar pill a powerful medicine. Belief leads sane people to do insane things. Belief can enable or diminish the human potential. The belief that it's okay to get even, almost a social more, is a destructive belief. Most of the beliefs many of us hold have been inherited. Often they are chicken-yard beliefs. Changing our beliefs may be the most empowering and most difficult aspect of personal growth. Self-limiting beliefs are exactly that—self-limiting. For years I have referred to such beliefs as "value norm anchor points," and they can truly be anchors. Webster defines *anchor* as "something that serves to hold an object firmly." Belief anchors exist everywhere. They arise from many facets of society.

They can be shown in popular sayings, even seen on bumper stickers, such as "Money is the source of evil" and "Thank God it's Friday." What do these beliefs do? TGIF essentially communicates how much we hate our work week. Characterizing money as evil says, "I like evil and want it" or "I don't want it!" Think about the sayings you know and perhaps use. What do they communicate? Do they speak of abundance? Do they address your real desires? In other words, do they serve you?

If prosperity is something you seek, will you obtain it if in the back of your mind is the idea that it will corrupt you—that you will become evil? If excellence in the work place, maybe a promotion, is what you seek, will TGIF get you there?

Most people hold beliefs that are mutually exclusive.

That is, they seek prosperity and believe that prosperity is evil. At some point in their lives, the conflicting beliefs challenge one another. Because this dissonance is typically unconscious, the stronger belief wins. The strength in our beliefs is strongest if fear is attached to it. So, the "biggest" fear wins. The marvelous book and movie *Harry Potter and the Prisoner of Azkaban* portray a scene in which the only magic that can overcome evil is derived by calling upon a powerful memory of joy and love. When Harry finds that love-joy mix, he is able to dismiss the evil, but only then. This is a powerful, true-to-life metaphor. The only force stronger than fear is love. Somehow, though, the John Wayne "Fill your hands, you sons o' bitches" metaphor is given more value in real life than "whatever you do unto the least of thy brethren." Why is that?

Again, it is the circularity of fear that perpetuates itself, and unfortunately, infects altogether too many people. Building self-worth then begins by examining both one's beliefs and one's fears.

Love is a soft word that would-be macho types could have difficulty dealing with. Love is not used here in the romantic sense but in an alternative sense to anger and fear. A helping deed done without an eye to reward is an act of love. A kind word is an act of love. A reassurance in time of need can be an act of love. Kindness is love.

Behind my former offices is a small waterway that handles runoff. It usually has some water in it year round. Birds gather there early in the morning to drink. I used to find there a gentleman every morning when I got to the office before 7 A.M. He had an old automobile and dressed in old clothes—but every morning he was there with two or more loaves of bread, feeding the birds. This one man has made this small area, perhaps a quarter of an acre, a unique heaven on earth for the local birds. His kindness is an act of love, but if you met him, a rather large, rough-looking man, you might be put off by background thoughts (beliefs), and it is unlikely you would see him as the gentle man he is. The word *love* may be out of vogue for those who need to prove something, but it never is for those who know who they are.

There are three basic elements to nonromantic, unconditional love. The first may surprise you. It is quite simply awe. Children fall in love with everything. Small children love the noise of a new toy, the motion of the wind, the majesty of a tall tree, and so on. They find awe in almost everything. Awe brings a glow to their faces and puts laughter on their lips. They can cry as though they have lost their dearest loved one when a toy breaks. Their innocence is not the lack of critical mental abilities as is so often thought. Their innocence truly sees the beauty, the joy, and the awe in so much of all that surrounds us each day. Awe is the realization that simple explanations do not begin to address the beauty of a rose, the words of a talented poet, the myriad of faces that smile back at a smiling face on a busy street. Awe is the wonderment that empowers and ennobles the human spirit. Awe recognizes the miracle behind every breath we take. Awe sees the glory of creation for what it is, an unexplained event of monumental, even ineffable, stature.

Unfortunately, our chicken-yard training tends to diminish awe with explanations, so we learn about Darwinian evolution and Big-Bang Theory, but our teachers fail to share with us that neither theory is proven or fact. They are but the modern, albeit scientific, stories we tell our young people, and of course, we scoff or laugh at myths taught generations ago that told the story differently. We are not told that only DNA can create DNA and that, according to some, the original elements necessary to create DNA did not exist in the soup present on earth when life supposedly just appeared from nothing.[36] We are not told the so-called Big Bang theory has undergone many revisions just to avoid the old "Prime Mover" arguments.

We learn many things this way, and therefore we dismiss their beauty and awe. We turn our lights on and enjoy the electric service, knowing where electricity comes from but failing to recognize that even science has never explained where electricity truly comes from. Oh, we can give an electron a name and explain most of its behavior, but electron jumps and other anomalies are simply left out of the teaching. If we don't understand it, the rule is, Ignore it. So long as something can be named, then a certain familiarity is born and, further, a sense of knowing what something is by knowing what it is called. This is not elegant nor is it a deliverance from the so-called noncritical abilities of a small child.

Awe is everywhere if we stop to sense the world around us. Love begins with a capacity for awe. Awe has many synonyms, including humility, and humility is a character asset that can be cultivated in our beliefs. The character aspects of each of us ennoble the human condition.

Another basic element in love is empathy. The trite but true saying "Unless you have walked in another man's shoes" is an outward expression of the empathy we can seek to encourage. Webster defines *empathy* this way: "the action of understanding, being aware of, being sensitive to, and vicariously experiencing the feelings, thoughts and experience of another" or "the capacity for this."

The third element is best stated in a question: Am I attached to the outcome? Unconditional love is not attached to an outcome. Giving love to another is not an instrument of negotiation. All those times you may have heard something like "If you loved me, you would___" may have unconsciously conditioned you to expect quid pro quo from love, but that kind of love is a quasicontractual obligation. Unconditional love is not bargained for. When given, it is not given with an eye to indebtedness. Unconditional love is just that—no expectation, no attachment to any outcome—simply love.

You may ask, as I once did, is it possible to give unconditional love? Is it possible to love someone—a child, for example— and not be committed to an outcome for that child? After all, parents want many things for their children. If the love is truly unconditional, then it survives even if the child leaves home and wants nothing to do with the parents. As in the biblical story of the prodigal child, the love remains. It is said that God loves us all this way, and where there may well be something God would have had us do differently, God's love never abandons us.

**True self-esteem comes from what we give,
not from what we take.**

In short, we build esteem by adding, not by subtracting, and we add most when we add from unconditional love. When we go to the aid of another, and do so without an eye to what we might get out of it, we add both to our worth and to the worth of mankind in general. When we give love without condition—a string attached, so to speak—we add again both to our worth and to that of another. True self-esteem comes from what we give, not from what we take. It comes from the walk we walk, not from the things we say. True self-esteem builds character, not ego. It is, after all, the act of being who we really have been created to be. Further, our intention to give unconditionally creates a field that generates opportunities beyond the scope of selfish intentions.

*** ***

Each of us is great insofar as we perceive and act
on the infinite possibilities which lie undiscovered
and unrecognized about us.
— James Harvey Robinson

CHAPTER TEN

You Deserve the Best You Possible:
It's Never Too Late

There are two questions I often hear. The first has to do with purpose. I hope by now you realize your purpose is service and life is a journey, not a destination. The second has to do with guilt and fear and even aging. Despite the many varieties in which I hear this question, it generally can be stated this way: "I think it's too late for me, and I don't deserve the best."

Your purpose is service and
life is a journey, not a destination.

Sometimes the "too late" has to do with age and sometimes with actions in life. I will tell you the same thing all sacred documents say: "It's never too late while you still draw breath." As long as you breathe, you are in motion. The entire universe is in motion, expanding and contracting—not all that different from your lungs. Without motion there is atrophy and stagnation or entropy and eventually singularity. When we do leave this plane, the moment we die nothing changes but breath. For a time, cells continue to divide and multiply and otherwise carry on in their local communities just as they did during what we call life. What's stopped is breath.

Thoughts are in motion. Our stream of consciousness, inner talk, is in motion. Our thoughts create and communicate. Even when physically unable to do certain things, our mind can do the doing. Research has shown how prayer from a stranger at great distance can heal. It is never too late!

Once, however, I too held the notion that it was too late for me. My awakening was slow. For a long time I refused to take a long serious look at myself. I ran from my own emotional pain and hid behind money, power, anger, hostility and false pride. But one day I couldn't hide any longer. Little by little the layers were peeled away until I was forced to seek my true self. I had lots of help along the way, and I guarantee you will too if you choose to make the journey, one that seems to know no end and leads over and over only to that question, "How high is up?" The Universe will provide you with rewards and help, as it did me, because that is simply how the Universe works. Dr. Wayne Dyer in his excellent work *The Power of Intention* puts it this way: "Intention is not something that you do, but rather a force that exists in the universe as an invisible field of energy." He continues, quoting Carlos Castaneda's work *The Active Side of Infinity*: "Intent is a force that exists in the universe. . . . those who live off the Source beckon intent, it comes to them and sets up a path for attainment."

You are not your mind or body—you are spirit.

According to Dr. Dyer, you cannot know the meaning of life until you connect with the power that created you. You are not your mind or body—you are spirit. Spirit is giving and creative. Spirit is kind, loving, beautiful, expanding, abundant, and receptive. Emulating these qualities begins the connection process.

Dyer also says that each of us is a God experience walking! I read this for the first time on an airplane flight, and I began to look at everyone differently. The Divine, by whatever name you prefer, creates every human being, who is therefore a Divine experience walking. I can't tell you how many smiles, rules bent, and other help I received while I held this vision of everyone I encountered: "You are a God experience walking."

Back to it's never too late. In my journey there came a point when I hungered for more metaphysical information. I enrolled in a California university, The University of Metaphysics, and by correspondence commenced a study in metaphysical science. This was not the metaphysics of an upper-division philosophy course, as I expected; rather, it was a practical metaphysics for living. I had worked for a long time, often doubling the required number of exams in order to reach their designated bachelor's level of education in this unique form of metaphysical science when they sent me the news. I was ready to advance, but to do so I must become an ordained minister.

This was not a strictly academic environment, and I should have recognized that, but the requirement blind-sided me. Still, I knew I was not worthy of being anyone's minister, including myself.

Weeks passed, and one Sunday afternoon while reading spiritual materials, I remembered a teaching from the school. I pulled out a binder in which I kept many notes, and the letter from the university fell upon the floor. As I picked it up, I knew immediately that I missed the lessons and all the joy and change they had brought into my life. I sat back down in my recliner and held the letter in my lap.

My thoughts put me to sleep, and soon I was dreaming. This is the dream.

> Once upon a time a man looked to himself. He spoke to himself, "I desire to serve God, but my life has been full of error. The example I have set is not that of a cleric. People will only scoff and say, 'Know ye them by the fruits of their tree.' Who am I, then, to speak for or of God?"
>
> With these words circling within his head, the troubled man lay down to rest. He spoke to God. "Your will, not mine, be done."
>
> As he drifted into sleep, pictures began appearing that told this story.
>
> Once there stood a tree—a tree of life, full of fruit. The limbs bent toward the earth under the weight of the lush red cherries. The cherries danced in jubilee with the breeze that bathed their tender skins and turned their

fullness and vivid color to face the Father, the Sun of the heavens.

With the dew and the rain they would polish their beauty and drink of the earth; to store within the energy and vitality of life taken from the soil through the roots and fired with the spirit of the Sun radiating through the leaves of their parent tree.

But alas, not all of the children of the tree would mature into lush red fruit. Out of an urge to experience and learn on his own, one turned away from the Father and ignored the parental warnings. Charlie, as he was known by the others, kept his life juices warm, daring the cold, the frost, the elements. He began to fill with color and mature early.

Pivoting on his base, he turned away from the Sun and took shade in the leaves. Daring to fornicate with the world, Charlie refused to release the natural pesticides within himself and took up affairs with the parasites.

Soon his delicate skin was broken, and his fruit exposed. The fragrance attracted the birds, and they too feasted on his flesh. Charlie lived off the flesh and of the world. Passion, experience, and knowledge were his prize.

Then one day the gardener came. Gently he took from the parent the pure and ripened children, leaving only Charlie behind. Hanging alone, Charlie looked about him. The fall nights were cold and lonely. His friends, the birds, were on wing, abandoning him. His flesh had spoiled, and even the insects avoided him now. His soul hung onto his tattered body. The elements he had once faced with a thrill now threatened to snap him from the stem of life. Charlie was sad and lonely. He had learned these things: knowledge is not necessarily wisdom; experience is not always a kind teacher; and passion is sometimes a poison that betrays whatever value there is to be had in experience and knowledge.

Charlie looked up at the beautiful blue sky and the buoyant white billowy clouds adrift, seemingly with nothing to do or a care in the world, lazily on sail across the vast blue heavens. "They and the lilies of the field," Charlie said to himself.

"Dear God," he spoke aloud, "I have sinned. I have wasted the beauty of your flower and turned my back on simple truth. In my pursuit of wisdom, I lost sight of Your Great Form and indulged in physical illusions. I was lost. I alone am to blame. I give my essence over to thee, Creator of all that is good within me and all that could ever be love within me. For you are **Eternal Love**, and what is best for me is also your way. That I should discover this so late in my life is my most significant regret.

"I have watched the caterpillar spin his cocoon and perch on the leaves above me as a butterfly," Charlie continued, "but I fear that this recognition has come so late in my life that I will be unable to share this Beauty, this Truth, with others."

With that Charlie lowered his head. Suddenly a squirrel jerked him from the limb and scampered down the tree and across the meadow. The squirrel paused, examined Charlie, and then as though rejecting him, dropped Charlie in the grass.

Charlie rested there for a day or two, and then the snow came. Covered by the white blanket, Charlie slept.

The seasons passed as though in the twinkling of an eye. Charlie took root and grew strong. From his branches came blossoms, followed by fruit more beautiful than Charlie could ever remember beholding.

Charlie praised and gave thanks to God!

The lowly man in my dream raised his head from slumber. His prayer had been answered. The Lord does not forsake man; man forsakes the Lord. Thy will, not mine, be done; for, after all, in their eternal boundless beauty, they are one and the same.

My life has changed since this dream. Today many faces provide that warm fuzzy feeling when I put my head on the pillow. I enjoy my family and the lovely bride to whom I have been married for more than sixteen years. In fact, my wife and I were to have only one child. I committed to spend the first six years of his life with him and work from my home. So, I moved offices to my home and had a wonderful time. I stopped traveling and lecturing and spent the time learning, writing, and administering a business. Then my youngest was born. He too was due the first six years. The long and short of it is that for twelve years I sort of disappeared. When I reentered the world, so to speak, I was astounded at how many people thought I had died. "I haven't seen or heard from you for so long, I thought you were dead," was not an uncommon line. Well, as that old saying goes, "Rumors of my death are greatly exaggerated."

Today I can honestly say that those twelve years enriched my life immensely. I do believe that everything happens for some reason. I have practiced the messages in this book and can say to you in heartfelt honesty, they work!

*** ***

I want to know God's thoughts.
All else are details.

— Albert Einstein

CHAPTER ELEVEN

The Kingdom Within

What if the world truly is magical? What if we were created to be co-creators with all the power to manifest miraculous lives if we but believed so? What if we were our own cheerleaders, full of encouragement and rah-rah support? A friend of mine, Terri Marie, wrote a marvelous little book all about being our own cheerleaders. The book, entitled *Be the Hero of Your Own Game,* suggests that we are usually good at encouraging others but then tell ourselves all the reasons why we cannot succeed. What if we believed that we were created with every good possibility in our hands to be the very best of ourselves, to use our unique talents and abilities in ways that might astound many, to have happiness, peace, balance, and harmony in every day in everything we do? What if our Father in Heaven looked upon us with the love and blessings that human parents have when they behold their newborn child and with His all-good, all-powerful, and all-knowing best offered all that He had to us?

What if we were created to be co-creators with all the power to manifest miraculous lives if we but believed so?

I believe that God, or whatever term you are comfortable with for the Creator, has done just that. Remember Mark Twain's story in his book *Letters to Earth?* The point of the story was, hide God where mankind will never look. Hide Him within man—the last place he will ever look!

While I was lecturing abroad, a wonderful man approached me with some questions. He had resigned his priesthood two years earlier because he felt inadequate. He recognized that he had provided help to many but was disturbed that he himself was not worthy to give good advice. His thoughts were not all pure, and besides, he too was born a sinner.

We spoke for some time. I asked him several questions. In the end, he admitted that no one could be worthy according to that which he had been taught. Like many, he had been trained to believe that the Grand Organizing Designer had created him imperfectly. He was born a sinner, here to endure with courage and faith the suffering that he would experience. Further, this very suffering was necessary for him to prove his devotion and love for God. Since he had been a Christian priest, training for twelve years as such, I asked him about some of the words of Jesus. According to Jesus, "The kingdom of heaven is within." Further, "My Father has many mansions. Why would you use my words and not do my deeds? All that I do, you will do and more. If you had faith but as tiny as a mustard seed." All of these quotations in context clearly suggest that God dwells within all of us. They also suggest that Christ consciousness is what we should all seek to achieve. Indeed, Jesus states very clearly that we are all his brothers and sisters. Nowhere does Christ suggest that we are poor pitiful creatures created to suffer. The message of Christ is love!

From here our conversation entered the domain of Christian mysticism and this led to the "I AM" presence. "I am that I am," spoken by God to Moses. The Great I AM presence is the kingdom of heaven, or God/Christ consciousness within. (This is a study worth undertaking but one that is beyond the scope of this work, so I suggest "The I AM Discourses" published by St. Germain Press if you wish to pursue this further.) I was then asked, "Is this the reason that all of your affirmations on InnerTalk programs begin with 'I am?'"

My mind flashed back to a small bookstore in Reno, Nevada, where nearly twenty years before I was asked the same question. "Actually," I answered, "the research shows this is the best way to state the affirmations. I do find it interesting that it is the declarative,

'I am.'" We then spoke of prayer. The ancient texts were often interpreted incorrectly. The word *ask,* when translated correctly, should read *declare.* Declaring is creating, not petitioning. At length we had traveled around the world and examined many religious systems. We agreed, whether Christ consciousness or Buddha consciousness, whether from the Upanishads or the Bible, whether Lao-tzu or Zoroaster, all the great living religions taught *love* at their core. Suffering as some creation made imperfectly and therefore unable to avoid sin, begging for salvation and so forth, was not the teaching. No—to the contrary, the GOD within created all with the ability to manifest miracles, if they but had faith the size of a tiny mustard seed.

It was then that the lights went on in the mind of my new friend. "Oh, I get it. When you teach people to suffer, even indirectly, you claim suffering for them and yourself. How could I have missed that? No wonder I always felt guilty and ashamed."

This gentleman has since made some remarkable changes in his life. He still helps people, but now he empowers them to help themselves. Through forgiveness, releasing guilt and blame and therefore shame, today he teaches the unlimited power within. All of this begins by taking responsibility for everything in our own life.

Earlier I suggested an acronym for fear. Let me suggest a couple more: False Evidence Appearing Real and Forget Everything And Run. You were not created imperfectly to fear the world or anything else for that matter. You are, as Dyer puts it, "A God experience walking."

When I suggested the forgiveness messages for our prison inmate population, there was some concern. After all, forgiveness sounds very much like grace. Accepting responsibility is fine, but forgiveness? Forgiving and forgetting, or letting go—what does that mean?

I was in my hotel room one evening when my host informed me that a gentleman had just flown in from Singapore to hear my lecture. Supposedly I had been an inspiration to his work, and he wanted to meet me. The arrangement was made, and I met Dr. Mel Gil, a wonderful man with a terrific sense of humor. Dr. Gil had lost an arm and loved to joke about it. He used for empowerment what many would consider a handicap. He gave me a copy of his book *Uncommon Sense.* That evening I read his book. In it I found a chapter entitled "Forgiving or Forgetting." Mel used a marvelous metaphor that adds to our understanding of forgiveness power. When you forgive, "Who are you giving to but yourself. . . . Forgetting when split into two words (equals) 'for getting.' What are you getting in response to forgiving other people? Well, you are getting freedom."

The Great I AM presence has already forgiven you, for as The Course in Miracles[37] points out, the real you, the Christ consciousness that is your quintessential self, is and has always been perfect, just as it was created. All you must do is accept that truth and everything changes. Or, as in the parable of the prodigal son, return (recognize) to the Father and His house and all is forgiven.

Life is a schooling process. Mistakes are teaching lessons. Remembering that and who you really are is awakening. There is a story about the Buddha that illustrates this point. It seems the Buddha was walking one day when he met a fellow traveler on the path. The traveler fell down at the feet of Buddha and proclaimed, "You must be God." The Buddha answered, "No, I'm not God." The traveler insisted, "Then you must be a demi-God!" Again the Buddha replied, "No, please get up. I'm not God or a demi-God." The traveler, confused, then asked, "Okay, tell me, what are you?" The Buddha answered, "Only awake."

This story always reminds me of the glorious book *Letters to Strongheart.* Strongheart was among the first animal movie stars. A German shepherd, Strongheart played the first real dog hero. When he passed over, his handler, J. Allen Boone, wrote a book that expressed imaginary letters to Strongheart with their replies from the other side. In one of these letters Strongheart states, as I recall, "What a hideous sight to behold faces as incomplete as minds."

Mel Gil has identified twelve ways in his book *Uncommon Sense* that people use to escape accountability. In statements they are expressed this way:

1. I'll try
2. If_____ then_____!
3. I forgot!
4. It's not my fault.
5. I had no choice.
6. I can't.
7. I had no control.
8. I'll wait and see.
9. I don't know!
10. It's not my job.
11. That's just the way I am.
12. Nobody told me.

Trying is not doing.

Those statements are all excuses. Trying is not doing. Conditional acts are waiting, not acting. Forgetting simply says it wasn't important enough for me to write down or remember. Not my fault is another way of blaming and escaping personal responsibility. No choice? What does that mean? Can't? Only if you believe you can't, and so forth. The bottom line is this: **You do have the power and the ability.**

Within you is an absolutely awesome potential. You deserve, and you are worthy. Your life begins each moment anew. It is never too late and it is always right to pursue your highest potential. It is all a matter of changing some old views. Perhaps, as with me, some tool like InnerTalk aids you in getting rid of those old, negative self-beliefs. Whatever your path and your tool, you are a miracle, and you do deserve happiness. You are here to learn—not to suffer. You are a gift from the Divine, and you were not created deficiently. There is nothing for you to feel shame over. Shame is a tool of guilt. It can be used to control you and force you to deny your real higher self.

What you've done in the past is a lesson, and when you understand that, accept and forgive yourself and all others, commit to your very best—all else is taken care of for you. The gifts have been given; they are there for you to accept. Again, you absolutely do have the power and ability to manifest peace, balance, and harmony in your life. You absolutely do have the power and the ability if you but believe.

Each of us is but one drop in the proverbial sea of being.

Process theologians use a metaphor or analogy when they speak of mankind and Creator. Just as each of the cells in your body is conscious in some way, your love and consciousness of them heal and protect all of you. You and I and all of us are analogously cells in the body of the Creator. Each of us is but one drop in the proverbial sea of being. Our Creator is conscious and loving of all of us; we need only to be conscious and loving to share in the co-creative powers endowed upon us by the act of creation. Eliminate the doubt, fear, shame, guilt, blame, and so forth and accept our true birthright. Rescript the old ANTs (Automatic Negative Thoughts), replacing them with positive loving thoughts full of acceptance and gratitude. Reach down inside now and see if this doesn't seem so familiar and so true as to be noetic—knowledge you have always known but perhaps forgot.

In the next chapter we'll take a look at what we might expect in our journey of self-empowerment—both the rewards and the disappointments—but first let me share a story with you about struggle. Personal growth or improvement involves change, and that can mean struggle. I recall a cute little book a few years ago that stated in its title, "Life was never meant to be a struggle." Perhaps that is so from a certain perspective, but for most of us, struggles are how we grow. Like the proverbial steel in the mill that grows stronger during the tempering process (heating, cooling, reheating, and so on), we grow stronger from our own struggles. So, struggle does not mean bad;

rather, it should equate with growth, and it does so when our lens of perception sees life's struggles in this way. Here is the story.

There once was a scientist who beheld the glory of an emperor moth and was so totally taken by the creature that he decided to study it. For more than a year he monitored the activities of the giant moth.

One day he came upon a caterpillar ready to spin its cocoon. He gently captured the caterpillar and took it back to his lab. He watched the caterpillar build its cocoon within a glass container and enter that state of deep sleep. While in the chrysalis it changed its form, from crawling on the ground to floating in the sky.

The day came when the moth was ready to leave the cocoon. The scientist watched anxiously as the tiny head chewed its way into the light of the laboratory. The moth struggled and struggled, seemingly getting nowhere. Its body was simply too large to fit through the tiny hole in the cocoon. The moth tired and laid its head to rest on the shell of the cocoon. The scientist took it upon himself to help the tiny creature. "How could I stand here for so many hours watching this beautiful moth go through such agony and pain?" he questioned. "Where is my mercy?" he continued as he took his tweezers and scissors to cut away the cocoon. The moth fell from the cocoon badly deformed, and soon died.

Later the scientist discovered that it was precisely the cocoon-escaping struggle that forced the fluids down into the body of the emperor moth and gave it its aerodynamic ability. The cocoon forced the fluids into the body, perfectly proportioning the moth as it forced its way out. Cutting away the cocoon in an effort to help had only killed the moth.

Struggle does not mean bad.

There are a couple of morals to this story. Sometimes what seems like a struggle is indeed creating improvement, and sometimes what might appear as helping is only making matters worse.

In the end, it's up to each of us as individuals to make the best of our lives. For me that means happiness, which begins with self-responsibility. Remember, you may not be in charge of everything in your world, but you are definitely in charge of your inner environment.

Now, as I promised, let's take a look at change.

*** ***

All that is necessary for the triumph of
evil is for good people to do nothing.
— Edmund Burke

CHAPTER TWELVE

Change

Change is perhaps the most sought-after goal in life. If we but had more money, more education, and less compulsion, could lose weight or stop smoking, be more popular and have more friends, and so forth, life would be perfect. Change is also perhaps the most frightening experience we can undertake. Change means giving up something, some belief, some habit, some pattern, some something. Change from the inside out can also mean great risk.

Genuine change often means letting go of acquaintances who hold different beliefs—like our bad-luck fortune-cookie carriers. It isn't so much that we let go of them as they abandon us, for we no longer provide a sanctuary safe for "cookie" sharing. There are also plenty of naysayers. Like the smart chickens in the chicken house, they will tell you all this is nonsense. Some may even attack you with such words as *hoax* and *fraud*. Like most attacks, they are designed to produce feelings of insecurity, doubt, even stupidity. One book out there suggests that self-help efforts generally rob people of their money and their esteem. The book is entitled *Sham: How the Self-Help Movement Made America Helpless,* by Steve Salerno. I heard him tell of a sales event he attended with salesmen all from the same company. He criticized the motivational speaker on the grounds that in the beginning of the presentation the speaker told everyone in the audience that each could be the number one salesperson in the coming year. Such was a logical absurdity, he asserted, for how could they all be number one in the same company? Stop and think about it for a minute. Do you really think either the salespeople or the motivator took this statement to mean anything other than each of the salespeople in the room had the ability to be number one? I don't. Indeed, I have been guilty of far worse, at least on the surface, by stating that we can win at everything!

We can win at everything.

Now you might say, "How is it possible to win at everything?" The answer is simple, but it is also involved in the definitions attached to winning and losing. Let me get this point straight, right from the beginning. We only lose when we let ourselves down! We can only win, in the real sense of winning, when we do our very best! Our very best requires commitment, courage, dedication, singleness of purpose or focus, and more. These attributes are fundamentally known as character.

A friend of mine, Coach Phil Porter, says, "The basis of winning is character." Phil is an ninth dan black belt in martial arts, a retired Air Force major, and the coach of many Olympic players. He adds, "Character is simply a combination of all the virtues which have been the basis of American life."

Character is a hallmark of great champions. Character is developed. Character requires an earnest effort to be, to live, to think, and to act according to a code of conduct that dictates honesty and integrity in all things. No higher act of honesty exists than that which is necessary in order to stand back and say, "I know I did my very best!" Self-honesty can be one of the most difficult characteristics, and yet the most rewarding, a person can ever develop. The words of Pythagoras ring as true today as ever:

"Above all else, know thyself!"

Words and truisms can be interesting. When I was very young, the words "all men are created equal" disturbed me. What on earth did this really mean? It was obvious to any child that all men were not indeed created equal. Adults who truly wished to settle my concern over this foolish matter gave me many answers. Their typical answer went something like "in the eyes of God, all men are equal."

Although this answer did provide some comfort, it nevertheless failed to register at every level of my being as "true." Then one day the answer was put to me another way. It went something like this: Imagine a rocket scientist who after much work launches an interstellar voyager. Imagine the pride he feels in the accomplishment. Now imagine a so-called menial laborer. On his hands and knees for endless hours, he scrubs and polishes a floor. He has worked so hard and with so much pride that he has scrubbed his knuckles raw. Now he stands back and beholds his labors. The floor absolutely glistens—every square inch of it. It never looked this good even when it was new. Now, I was further instructed, which man senses the most pride, the rocket scientist or the floor scrubber?

Even at a young age, I recognized that questions such as this one were obvious. If both men did their absolute very best and knew it, put their whole heart, mind, and soul into their work, their pride of accomplishment would be equal. To the degree that they compromised their very best, to that precise degree their sense of accomplishment would be diminished.

In this day and age, change can also mean risking reputation and even our livelihoods. Is it unscientific to include the spiritual component in science? I don't think so. Again I hark back to a word of William James: *pragmatic*. Is science capable of investigating pragmatic outcomes? The answer is clearly yes.

I have experienced personal attacks for some of my work and know first-hand that when we stand outside the established norm (establishment), we may find ourselves standing alone, at least for a while. I am also fortunate to know many that stood with me and supported my work, even in the darkest hours. Today the technology and methods I have discussed for changing a person's inner beliefs, known now as InnerTalk®, have been demonstrated effective in dozens of studies. Today the mind-body-spirit connection is so well established that denying it is absurd. Still, whenever individuals ask me to recommend a health care professional who will treat them holistically rather than mechanically, I remember just how short in supply these professionals are, and then I think of Dr. Cristian Enescu.

Dr. Enescu is a prominent neurologist in New Jersey whom I have the great pleasure of knowing. Rather than tell you about him, I will let his own words, shared with my office in an interview, tell his own story. My wife, Ravinder, wrote the introduction and conducted the interview.

For several years now, Dr. Enescu has been sharing InnerTalk with his patients and periodically would call us to share some of his amazing stories. We are thrilled that he managed to find time in his busy schedule to work on this interview with us.

Why did you choose to become a doctor?

Mathematics was my best subject in high school, and I had thought that I would become a mathematician or engineer. However, during my last year of high school, an "inner voice" was telling me that I should choose a career in which I could "help" people. It was because of this "inner voice" that I started pursuing medicine as a career.

Where did you get your training?

I graduated with honors from medical school in Bucharest, Romania, in 1983. Six years later I moved to Greece for just under a year, where I worked as a researcher. In 1990 I moved to the United States, and after working as a research associate in the neurology department at the City of Hope Medical Center in California, I entered an internship program at Brookdale University Center in Brooklyn, New York. I then went on to do my neurology training at St. Vincent's Hospital in Manhattan.

Why did you become a neurologist?

During my year in Greece, I had the privilege of meeting a prominent Greek neurologist, Spyros Skarpalezos. We spent a great deal of time discussing neurology. Then during my first year as an intern, I met another neurologist, Miran Salgado, who explained to me the spiritual aspect of neurology. You see, neurology deals directly with the brain, the brain and the mind are inseparable, and the mind plays an important role in all healing. So, while as a doctor I could help people, as a neurologist I could maybe discover how my patients could use their own minds to help in their own healings. Neurology allows me not only to understand how my patient's brain is functioning but also gives me the opportunity to study and experiment with my own brain.

How did you first hear about InnerTalk?

During my first year as an intern, my life was busy—too busy! I needed to find ways to relax and to speed up my own recovery process so that I could function better. I searched the Internet and came across InnerTalk. I was amazed by what I read. If the information were really true, then InnerTalk had to be really important for all mankind. Of course I had to try this technology for myself. The first programs I tried were *I Am Relaxed, Using Both Halves of the Brain,* and *Synchronicity.* What I found was that previously I had known nothing about relaxation. The InnerTalk programs helped me to relax more deeply and made me aware of a much greater reality. My InnerTalk programs became my personal oasis of quietude. I went on to get many more programs, and I benefited from all of them.

What were the benefits you gained from InnerTalk?

I am an avid reader and had learned about deeper states of relaxation, which lead to a heightened awareness of reality, but I had been unable to achieve this. With InnerTalk I was finally able to put into practice what I had previously only heard about. I then started exploring the more spiritual programs, such as *Opening Up to a Higher Power* and *Using the Force,* and I worked through the *Self-Hypnosis* course. However, it was the *Path to Mastership* library that truly changed my life. You see, before using InnerTalk, I was a successful doctor, but there was no depth or real meaning to my life—there was no spiritual connection. I felt that there had to be something else in this life—something was missing. Since using InnerTalk, my life has changed dramatically. I found new joy in living, and my life became a fascinating adventure, like a huge jigsaw puzzle with pieces falling into the right places one by one.

In my practice everyone noticed the change in the message I was delivering to my patients. The financial aspects of my practice, though still important, became completely eclipsed by the daily search to find ways to awaken my patients' minds. My purpose for becoming a doctor was not just to be successful but also to truly help people, and now I feel I am doing just that.

With InnerTalk I was finally able to put into practice what I had previously only heard about.

When and how did you start introducing your patients to InnerTalk?

I had experienced so many personal gains from using InnerTalk that I wanted to teach my patients about this wonderful tool. Of course, this is not promoted by the mainstream medical system, which wants to preserve itself. Physicians are expected to prescribe only drugs. All other alternative ways of healing are discouraged. In my case, I provide my patients the standard neurological care, and then I offer my own insights about mind healing. I had already made the observation in my own patients that those patients who were optimistic simply got better quicker and depressed patients got worse, regardless of the treatment protocols used.

Behind my desk, my patients see a large sign that reads: "Every day, in every way, I am getting better and better." During each exam, I make sure I am playing an InnerTalk program with gentle music. My patients feel more relaxed, and I explain to them the importance of being in a healing atmosphere. I then explain the importance of the mind in self-healing. The sign on my wall is there because of some work done by a French hypnotist. He found that patients who repeated this affirmation every night got physically better, while those in the control group did not experience the same gains. I tell all my patients about this research and other such studies. I then go on to explain to my patients that InnerTalk is one of the most powerful tools to access the power of their own minds. Most people have no idea how much control their subconscious minds have over their lives.

"Every day, in every way,
I am getting better and better."

There are some older people, maybe because of their mental decline, who are not as open to these ideas, so I do not go into these new ideas in much depth. However, their families invariably are interested, so I do discuss it with them. The fact is the mind is powerful, and the mind is capable of healing the body. Health care is a team effort. As the doctor I can run the test and prescribe the medicine, but the patient must take responsibility for being positive and for creating his or her own health. I teach all my patients how to use guided imagery to picture themselves well. This technique is cheap, has no side effects, and is incredibly powerful.

With everything I teach my patients I explain the importance of being consistent and patient. Some of my patients tell me that they will try these new techniques, and I tell them not to "try" but to "do." Some of my patients want to know exactly how quickly they will see the results of these techniques. I tell them that it all depends on how much effort they put into it. Not that playing InnerTalk programs takes effort, as you simply play it in the background. But you do need to put the program in your player and turn it on! I recommend that they use the nature format at night while they sleep and the music as much as possible during the day.

I should tell you, too, as I tell all of my patients, that I have no financial incentive to tell people about InnerTalk. I do not do it for money—I do it because I believe in InnerTalk and its ability to access the power of the mind.

How responsive were your patients to these new ideas?

Some patients are very responsive to these ideas. They put into practice all I have taught them, and they get better. When they want to thank me for the benefits they have realized, I have to explain to them that the merits go to them. It is the power of their own minds that has led to their health improvements.

In some instances, patients may be afraid even to own up to the power of the mind. They simply do not want to deal with the possibility that they may be able to heal themselves. To acknowledge that is to acknowledge that maybe they created the sickness in the first place. You have to be honest with yourself before you can access the power of your own mind. In these instances I tell my patients to watch for the signs. The fact is, we all encounter instances when what we expected to happen does in fact happen. If we expect the worse, we often receive just that. If we expect the best, then that is often what we get. I will also suggest some books or movies that may help them to become more open to the ideas I am trying to teach them.

For most people, life is like going to the theater where they are merely spectators. When you learn meditation, you will find that you are a part of the movie and that you have more control over how your story unfolds. I believe that meditation and spiritual awareness can help all of us live much more fulfilling lives. I also emphasize that it is one thing to read about spirituality and meditation and quite another to actually experience it for yourself. I tell my patients not just to talk about it but also to actually go and do it. This way they can become part of the action themselves.

However, I do have to respect my patients' time. Some people simply are not ready for such radical thinking. These patients I simply treat with "traditional" methods, and while I am able to help them, they do not see the same gains as the other patients.

You obviously see spirituality as an integral part in self-healing. How do you explain these ideas to an atheist?

Much scientific work has demonstrated the power of the mind. Many experiments in physics have shown that the outcome of experiments is dependent on the expectations of the observer. You simply cannot reject the practical role of the mind. If someone does not believe in a higher power, then I approach him or her from a very scientific point of view. The studies on the mind are reproducible and therefore totally scientific. It is therefore easy for me to change my approach from that of mysticism to hard science.

The studies on the mind are reproducible and therefore totally scientific.

What advice do you have for our readers?

Don't just believe me—do it for yourself. Once you have your own proof, then no one can take it away from you.

How do your colleagues respond to your approach?

I knew that I was doing something right, so it did not matter to me what my colleagues thought. My colleagues are afraid to bring spirituality into their work. They are afraid of bringing in new ideas as they may fail and so lose patients. Doctors are generally financially secure, and if they were to believe in InnerTalk and in the power of the mind, then they would have to change. Change means taking a risk, and generally doctors do not want to take risks with their own security. Very few doctors are open to the power of the mind. I have had a few patients who were not open to these new teachings, and some of my colleagues say that I should stop teaching it as I could lose these patients. But I am not a doctor so that I can keep patients; I am a doctor so that I can help people. The fact is, if an American president is elected with 60 percent of the popular vote, it is considered a landslide victory. If I can get 60 percent of my patients to take some responsibility for their own health, then I have been successful! As it is, my approach is not losing me any patients. On the contrary, I am doing even better than before!

Change means taking a risk.

Do you have any specific stories you can share with us?

One patient I was seeing had been suffering from migraines. Ten different doctors had given her the same medications, and they had never worked. When I saw her, I prescribed the same pills. This time they worked. She was surprised. I had to ask her if it was possible that it was not the medications she had taken but rather the other changes I had asked her to implement. I then suggested that she discontinue the medications but continue with the other practices. She is now free of migraines and free of medications. The InnerTalk programs I had her use were *Forgiving and Letting Go, Headache Relief, Healing and Releasing Emotional Pain* and *Freedom from Fear, Doubt, Helplessness, and Hopelessness.*

Another patient came to me suffering from multiple sclerosis. I told her that in order to get better, she needed not only to continue with her medications but also to pay attention to everything else that I had taught her. She started working with *Powerful Immune, Self Healing Is Natural, Freedom from Depression,* and *I Am Relaxed.* I think that the depression program is particularly important. Patients are often depressed and expect their condition to get worse. I believe that self-healing must start with the expectation that you can get well. This particular patient worked hard to implement all I had taught her. She tried to think positive even while she did not feel any better. Eventually it paid off. She no longer uses her cane and is optimistic about her future. She knows that she will get better, and she tells everyone this. She even went back to dancing, and the quality of her life has improved immensely. Now she tells everyone about the power of the mind!

**Self-healing must start with the
expectation that you can get well.**

I am also seeing great results with stroke patients. One of my patients, with weakness in the left side, experienced significant improvements in his walking and speech after using the InnerTalk programs in conjunction with his "traditional" treatment. His condition improved sooner than similar patients who had not used InnerTalk.

I get similar results with patients with Parkinson's. When they use InnerTalk while taking their medications, they get better faster, their tremors improve, and their anxiety levels are reduced.

**Basically my patients get better faster
when they use InnerTalk in addition to the
rest of their treatments, as compared
with similar patients who use only
the "traditional" treatment methods.**

Do you find the doctors or the nurses more open to the concept of the power of the mind?

Nurses are definitely more open to the power of the mind. They deal with the patients from the practical side. They see that the patients who are happier get better faster. They hear me explaining the power of the mind to my patients, and it makes sense to them.

Doctors, however, start practicing after a very long training, and they are already mentally tired and want to finally relax. Because of this, they are less inclined to embark on another type of training, a training that is totally different, the training in spirituality, even though this may be the most important training of their lives.

There is a gradually increasing pressure on the medical profession from insurance companies and the malpractice crisis. The system has become so complex and so sophisticated and is drawing all the energies towards the material aspects of their lives. As a result, physicians are less and less inclined to focus on the spiritual aspects of their lives. Also, physicians do not have a clear understanding of what meditation even is. They perceive meditation as just another way to relax, the same as having a drink by the pool with friends and family. They simply do not see the training of the mind as being important. They have no idea what they are missing.

Why do you believe meditation to be so important?

We cannot progress with spirituality without learning about meditation. Meditation is so much more than just relaxing, and it is different from praying. I was brought up as a Greek Orthodox Christian, and they believe in praying a lot. However, I see praying as "speaking to God," whereas meditation is "listening to God." Most people simply do not want to spend time working on something that seems so ambiguous, but the rewards are there for those who do.

Which programs do you think everyone should have in his or her personal library?

I think everyone should learn the true meaning of relaxation. Once you learn this, you can turn to the deeper levels of spirituality. I would therefore start everyone with the *Deep Relaxation* collection and then follow up with titles such as *Opening Up to a Higher Power* and *Connecting with the*

Force. I really like the *Platinum Plus* collection, especially *Manifesting Your Vision* and *Dream Petitioning.* I think that the *Path to Mastership* is the crown jewel in the InnerTalk line. This should definitely be in everyone's library. It is the most powerful program and works so well for the busy lives we all now live. I also use *Energy Meditation* and *Conscious Expansion,* and I think *Hyperemperia* is a must for everyone.

Are you saying that everyone should work with the spirituality programs, regardless of what their major issues are?

Most of my patients want specific results right away, but I believe that the true solutions lie in spirituality. I therefore use a combination of programs, some that are specific to a particular problem and some that deal with spirituality. This way they can see the immediate results while they work on the long-term solution that prevents the problem from coming back. It is only by reestablishing the mind-body connection that we can prevent the problems from recurring.

Are there any other titles you think we should carry in our line?

Your library is so extensive that I can always find a program that fits my needs and my patients' needs. I do not think you need to add to the line. What we need to do is tell more people about this technology. I truly believe that InnerTalk has the capability to change human civilization. It is so powerful and so needed that I think it should be in every hospital. The doctors would be able to relax so much more, and the patients would all recover faster. There is no one who cannot benefit from InnerTalk. InnerTalk truly is the tool for self-realization, and it is the best investment you could ever make. It is the best investment I have ever made, as it has changed my family life, my patients, and my professional life. I tell everyone about InnerTalk, but I am also very aware that I can only plant the seeds. I am not responsible for the germination.

Thank you, Dr. Enescu. I am sure that, like me, all of our readers have found your interview inspiring, enlightening, and educational. I wish more doctors had your dedication to truly helping their patients. I for one would be more comfortable about going to see a doctor who lived by your philosophy.

Let me share with you some other stories from people seeking improvement in their lives who have worked with InnerTalk. These represent a partial source of some of my own warm fuzzy feelings, but hopefully you will relate to at least one and gain the confidence necessary to take that step called change. We have run the studies, dozens of them, as I mentioned earlier. Still, there is truth in the words of Nathaniel Emmons: "Any fact is better established by two or three good testimonials than by a thousand arguments."

"I deserve!" They are the two most life-changing and most precious words in the English language. When you say, "I deserve" and really mean it in your heart, your life will change forever, permanently, and for the better! When you feel that "you deserve," you will no longer eat yourself senseless and numb, because you know that "you deserve" to treat yourself with kindness and with compassion. When you feel like "you deserve," you will honor yourself and respect others and no longer be a doormat for the convenience of friends and family. When you state loudly and proudly to the Universe, to God, and to the angels that "you deserve," you open yourself up to unlimited possibilities. I know what I am talking about!

A few years ago my life was a living hell, but once I summoned the courage and told myself that I do indeed "deserve" better, my life was on the road to healing and to new discovery! With the help of Eldon Taylor and his InnerTalk tapes and CDs, I was able to transform my life from the **inside out**!

I was once trapped in an abusive marriage, thinking I deserved to be treated like dirt. I weighed 350 pounds and ate all of my frustration and my rage. I knew deep down that I was smart, funny, and could do anything, but I was verbally beaten down so badly, I forgot who I was.

That all changed the moment it hit me that "I really do deserve." No one could take this step for me! I had to reach out for help, and Eldon Taylor had the tools for the inner change that I was praying for! The very first tape that I ordered was *Weight Loss Now*. I thought that being fat was my problem, but being obese was just a symptom of my low self-esteem. I listened to the tapes religiously, and slowly I began to see a change in how I viewed food. I began losing weight, and I gained more self esteem, but I still felt like I needed more encouragement. This time I ordered *Releasing Co-Dependent Patterns*. I learned that my husband could not abuse me without my permission, and once I withdrew my permission, my life really started to take off! For the first time in a long while, I felt worthwhile and worth the work that I was doing to change my behavior.

I continued listening to the tapes, and I added to my InnerTalk library. I ordered *Soaring Self-Esteem, Personal Power, Releasing Anger,* and the most powerful tape in my arsenal, *Ending Self-Destructive Patterns*. I slowly was changing and finally had the courage to divorce my husband and to take on my own life. You see, when you decide to take personal responsibility for yourself, and for your actions, you become your own hero! I finally realize that I had the power all along but needed the help from Innertalk tapes to help me along on my journey!

When I listened to these fine tapes, I found out that I was living under false programming—false programming that I was calling **my life**! I took the first step and called Dr. Taylor for help. Now I am happier, healthier, calmer, thinner (150 pounds lighter), but most important—I feel whole!

Now, it is up to you to realize that you can take on your own personal power and to take on your life. I know that sometimes you only feel a glimmer of what your life could be like . . . but hold on! Be true to your real self, and reach out to Dr. Taylor and his very kind staff. They are more than willing to help you along your new and very exciting journey of self discovery. You are a loving, capable, funny, smart, and worthwhile person. You deserve the best that life has to offer! Stop settling for less than what the real you can give! Life isn't meant to be tolerated and to be suffered through. Life is to be lived, with excitement and joy! Start taking responsibility for your own health, wealth, and happiness. Believe me, the journey will be worth it!

Jackie Howell, Utah

I'm writing to let you know how absolutely thrilled I am with the results achieved with the InnerTalk products. My journey began with *Self-Esteem, Success, Prosperity,* and *Self-Confidence.* My results came rapidly as I don't do things by halves and initially used the CDs for extended periods of time on a recurring basis. The results have been amazing. These products have definitely changed the quality of my life. I feel so much more joy, happiness and gratitude—my confidence is sky high—my outlook is totally optimistic, I am razor sharp and focused and constantly visualize only the best. The actions required to achieve my goals are now performed almost automatically, and as a result my business has improved dramatically. I honestly feel I have come to a place now where I am unstoppable and anything is possible. My advice to anyone looking to achieve improvement in any area of their lives is to try the products for themselves. I warmly congratulate Eldon Taylor on his accomplishments and contribution in the area of self-development and personal growth. **These products work!**

Daniel Calleja, Australia

The first time I invested in the InnerTalk CDs, I was a bit skeptical. I just went ahead and told myself to give it a try. After continually playing the CDs, I can see and feel the changes that are happening around me.

I found myself being more confident, having the ability to make decisions more constructively, and more positive vibes circulate around my environment.

The effect is more apparent in my daughter. She has matured faster and shows signs of vast developmental skills compared to her peers.

Overall, after five months of listening to the CDs, I must say there is indeed a positive improvement in our lives. Thank you.

Ranjit Singh, Malaysia

I first learned about the power of the mind when I was a teenager. After learning that I could change my life by changing my thoughts, I began to guard my thoughts more carefully and, most important, I started taking the time to monitor what was going into my mind. Knowing that my subconscious mind has the power to shape my destiny, I started looking for ways to put more positive ideas into my subconscious mind. One day I was fortunate enough to hear about Eldon Taylor's subliminal tapes. Since then, I have been hearing his tapes and CDs regularly in the areas of *weight loss, self-esteem,* and *prosperity.* As a result of hearing these wonderful subliminal recordings, I have lost and kept off 35 pounds, my self-esteem has risen considerably, and my prosperity knows no limits. I am constantly blessed by good things happening to me as a result of the prosperous thoughts my mind has been programmed with. About eight months after my daily practice of hearing Eldon Taylor's *Prosperity and Abundance* subliminal tape, I was fortunate enough to win $50,000 in my state lottery, which I used to pay for laser eye surgery and to take care of other obligations I had at the time.

Since then, I have prospered in business and in my social life, and I attribute this good fortune to the continual use of these products because dedicated use has allowed me to replace my old self-limiting thoughts with healthy, vibrant, and more creative thoughts, which have spilled out into every aspect of my life and continue to bless my life each day. These days I dedicate my free time to speaking and teaching others about the prosperous power of creative thinking, and I regularly give out Eldon Taylor's tapes at various seminars I give a few times a year. Some of my friends have told me about how these products have changed their lives, and I owe it all to the power of the subconscious mind.

Eddie Coronado, California

Before I started working with the InnerTalk programs, I felt like a rapidly aging 51-year-old spinster—gaining weight and going through the menopause. I just assumed life would be downhill all the way from then on.

I came across the InnerTalk programs quite by accident and decided to use them on myself as an experiment before I would think about using the programs in my complementary medicine practice. At that time, I was keen to change where my life was going, both physically and mentally.

The first CD I used was *Using Metabolism to Melt Fat*. I had not "dieted" as such for 25 years, as I know that dieting makes you fat by lowering the metabolic rate. Also, in the past, I never lost weight where I needed to—from my middle and legs—but only from my bust. However, my weight had crept up over the years from 8 stone 4 lbs (116 pounds) in my 20s and 30s to a whopping 10 stone (140 pounds). I thought realistically, I might get down to 9 stone 3 pounds (129 pounds—the maximum recommended weight for my height of 5'0").

How wrong I was! Amazingly, after listening to the CD for 6 weeks, I lost 7 pounds with no change in eating pattern.

Even more amazingly, it came off my waist and legs. I then stopped listening to the CD and have never used it since. I realized, however, that I was still losing weight, around 3 or 4 pounds over 6 months. One year after first listening to the CD, I weighed in at 9 stone 2 pounds (128 pounds). I then lost another 10 pounds rather too quickly while moving.

For the first time in my adult life, I have a normal hip-waist ratio and am no longer "blob-shaped." I have maintained my weight at 8 stone 4 pounds to 8 stone 7 pounds (116 pounds to 119 pounds) for more than 2 years now. The only problem is eating enough to prevent further weight loss. (I do not want to be too skinny.) Hardly any weight came off my bust, my hips are down from 34" to 33", I've lost 5" or 6" from my waist, and my legs are quite a "normal" size.

I believe the CD has permanently "re-jigged" my metabolism at a time in my life when I thought the middle-age spread was inevitable. Though I am back to the weight I was when I was younger, it is distributed in a much better shape. My friends are all amazed.

Since then I have used a number of different InnerTalk programs. I had suffered from headaches for years, so decided to use the *Freedom from Headaches*. As soon as I started to use the CD, I felt a pleasant tingling in my head and a calm feeling. Every time I use the CD, I notice when I look in the mirror how relaxed and soft my face looks—better than a facial. The headaches disappeared and have not returned. Nowadays I do get the odd headache, but nowhere near as severe, and the CD soon sees them off.

For years I had wanted to move, but it seemed impossible. I was afraid of being stuck in a chain, or being "gazumped" [someone making a higher offer] after incurring legal expenses, etc. My little daydream was that I would go view a house. The vendor, a lady on her own, would take a shine to me, announce that she wanted me to buy her house and no one else. She would then take it off the market so no one could gazump me. Meanwhile a cash buyer, a man, would knock on my door and offer to buy my house. There would be no "chains" involved . . . if only!

That was the dream, but it would need a miracle in a cut-throat, overheated housing market. I started to listen to *Expect a Miracle*. Two months later, I saw a suitable house and . . . it was exactly as in the dream! It all actually happened—the lady vendor, the cash buyer—as in the dream.

There was inevitably some stress attached to the move; my hair really suffered. I had always been known for my long, thick, curly hair. As the menopause approached, it became thin, dry with a few gray hairs, and the curl seemed to have gone. With the house move, it started thinning at an alarming rate; the hairdresser said there was nothing I could do about it and cut quite a lot off. How wrong he was. After the first few plays of *Freedom from Hair Loss,* there was a strong, pulling sensation on my scalp. After a few days when I washed my hair, the curls sprang back. I can honestly say my hair has never thickened up so quickly or grown so fast as over the next few weeks. One or two friends asked if I had started to color my hair because even the few gray hairs seemed to vanish. When I next went to the hairdresser, he was amazed at the difference in the quality and strength of the hair and could not believe that a CD could do this.

Last year I fell downstairs and damaged my shoulder very badly. The pain was severe and constant, night and day, for the first few months. I spent all my days for the first few months lying down. Even the Magnessage (bio-magnet) scarcely touched it. I found if I could get into one position and listen to *Natural Pain Relief,* by the time the CD finished I would be very comfortable and get some sleep. Without the CD I would have needed painkillers—something I prefer to avoid.

Although I do not suffer from inhalation allergies, some of my clients have an allergy to my cats. I therefore played *Freedom from Allergies* when treating those clients. I found that while I was playing this CD, my breathing became deeper and more relaxed, and my clients noticed an improvement in their allergy response.

Two friends used the *Natural Breast Enlargement* CD, both in their 50s. One "gained an inch" in 6 weeks. The other "went up a cup size." Both say their breasts are firmer and younger looking.

Although I am qualified in various therapies and pretty good on basic medical sciences, I always just bluffed my way through chemistry modules. Thanks to a good memory I could regurgitate the textbook on command, but I never really "got it." When I put the *Concentration* CD on while I was studying, it was as if a combination lock suddenly opened in my brain, and the basic concepts of chemistry were blindingly simple. I finally "got it" and can now handle the subject with ease.

I had always believed that being rich was not a good thing and felt slightly uncomfortable in wanting to have money when there were so many people in the world less fortunate than myself. However, after using the *Prosperity and Abundance* program, I found myself thinking about this in a different way. Now I believe that if, or rather when, I become rich, I will have the resources to help people.

I had an interesting experience when playing *Opening and Balancing the Chakras* during a massage session—the client suddenly said she could see colors. Although I never use the CDs without explaining what they are and obtaining consent, I had not actually told her what specific one had just started to play. The next time I saw her, she immediately recognized the CD as the same one because once again she could see these colors.

Releasing Anger always makes me feel very calm and relaxed when I listen to it.

All in all, using the InnerTalk CDs has helped me to move with relative ease; my friends all say that I am more confident; the excess 20 pounds has stayed off, giving me a better figure than when I was younger, and my hair has gone back to its thicker, curlier, premenopausal state. I am now 54 years old and feel much younger. I used to be pessimistic but now I am optimistic.

Best of all, I still have several more InnerTalk CDs waiting to be explored—they are my most valued possessions.

Thank you!

Elizabeth Christie, United Kingdom

I have been using Innertalk products for more than a year now, and I am still benefiting from them. I would not have done so well in juggling my life without the help of InnerTalk. A few of my regular topics are *Concentration, Powerful Memory, Accelerated Learning and Study, Power Learning and Memory, Time Management,* and *Relaxation.* I feel that I have so much enthusiasm to learn at school, and I am surprised to find myself having so much energy to keep up with my busy schedule. Life in New York is hectic, especially now that I'm in the nursing program for becoming a registered nurse. Health professions in the U.S. are not easy. It was very competitive just to get in, and now I have to worry about staying in the program. We have lots of homework, exams with high passing grades, and long clinical rotation hours. However, I feel relaxed and calm, and I always know what to do to keep myself on schedule and also at the same time to stay healthy. I realize that I am not as panicked and fearful as I used to be.

In the past, the block that I had was self-limitation. Lack of self-esteem, fears, and worries were the major things that limited my success. Now, I have confidence in myself. I also have noticed my improvement in writing papers after listening to *Creative Writing.* I was never fond of written assignments; they are my worst nightmares. Though I am still not very much interested in them, I can handle them much better now. I worry less, and I now hand in my papers on time. I can even concentrate better in generating my ideas. So far, I have done very well on all of them. Thank you, InnerTalk, for helping me to help myself. And I thank myself for having taken the initiative to try out the products.

Joon Theen Ng, New York

Jeron has a strong desire to represent his school for basketball competition. However, because of his physique and height, chances look rather slim. Knowing how the other Innertalk *Learning* CDs have helped him in his learning attitude and performance, Jeron started listening to the *Basketball* CD to perfect his skills. Barely two weeks later, his perfect shooting skills, baseline to baseline, etc., has earned him a place on the school team, and he is of course playing competitive basketball right now. Thanks to InnerTalk *Basketball* and *Winning Sports Performance*.

Jodee, Jeron's sister, has also used *Winning Sports Performance* to garner her strong win in the Junior Girls' Open (under 10) Table-Tennis Tournament organized by the Singapore Sports Council. She emerged as Top 8 in the national competition, though she was relatively new to this game and it was her first competitive experience. Her strong mental attitude, sporting and winning spirit, perfect performance, instinctive and natural playing, concentration, strong enthusiasm—empowered and enhanced via Innertalk *Winning Sports Performance* CD —have certainly enabled her first competitive winning track record. Jodee is looking forward to the release of *Table-Tennis* CD from Eldon Taylor to enhance the specific table-tennis skills/strokes for her future endeavors in her competitive journey.

Mr. and Mrs. Bonny Kua, Singapore

I just finished Eldon Taylor's new book, *Choices and Illusions*, which makes a strong case for subliminal learning documented by numerous case studies. I was so taken by this offering and the possibilities it offers concerning reprogramming our minds and bodies by listening to InnerTalk subliminal recordings that I immediately ordered and read one of his earlier books, *Subliminal Learning,* and several InnerTalk CDs. The second book gave me more information about the technology, and the CDs I am listening to regularly.

Either I am highly suggestible or these things actually work. Since listening to *Neat and Tidy,* which I am not, I find myself cleaning and picking up. When I listen to *Powerful Memory,* old memories from long past crop up as if my mind was defragging itself like a computer, and I have a compulsion to do a better job of remembering names, something that was not my forte. I haven't had the CDs for very long. I am going to keep playing them.

Winston Cook, Idaho
Co-author, *Incidents Beyond Coincidence*

I had a tournament going on so I began listening to the Innertalk *Basketball* CD. At that point, the team and I had no training sessions prior to the tournament, so the whole group has been kind of rusty. I noticed that I was improving in every match and doing more things that I usually would not have done. My performance seemed as if I had been training every day; even my coach was surprised. I was also surprised and happy that I haven't made any mistakes during my games. My confidence was very high, and I was very focused during the games. I'm very impressed at the short span of time and speed of change/results achieved by simply diligently listening to the InnerTalk CD.

Adrian Teng, Singapore
(former member of national team)

Three and a half years ago I first started using Eldon Taylor's InnerTalk programs. I was working as a booking agent for music acts, and most of the time I just did not feel very capable. I felt like something was wrong, but I did not know what it was. I felt afraid to move ahead and was aware of the negativity inside but did not know how to deal with it. I had been through the

12-step program for success, had tried using positive affirmations on myself, but nothing had worked. I still felt incomplete, as though there was much more that I could achieve in my life if only I could break through some elusive barrier.

When I first heard about subliminal programs, I was optimistic. I thought I had finally found the technology that could unlock the successful version of myself that was trapped inside. Unfortunately, I did not feel any change with the first subliminal programs I tried. However, I still felt that positive subliminal affirmations could hold the answer. Maybe the first company I had tried had an inferior product and there was more to creating an effective subliminal program than just burying the affirmations under the music.

Then I received a flier from a local company that spoke highly of a particular brand of subliminal programs, InnerTalk. I phoned the company to get more details and managed to get the phone number for Progressive Awareness, the publishers of InnerTalk.

When I called Progressive Awareness, the customer service representative explained to me the importance of choosing the right program for my particular goal. In discussing my story with her, I decided that what I needed was extra enthusiasm in order to carry through. I was also told that if I played the programs continuously, then I should be aware of some changes taking place within a few days.

I decided to work with *Ultra Success,* and within a few days I noticed that my self-talk had changed from "I can't" to "I can." I found I could picture myself being successful in a big business. I began to feel as though I could overcome any obstacle and find the answer to any problem. I now knew that success in my business meant working smarter, not harder, and I felt up to the challenge. My successes continued, and everyone could see the change in me. Obstacles that I was once afraid of I now had the confidence to handle. My fears were gone, I was making decisions, and I was solving problems, both at work and with my friends. I no longer felt intimidated and found it easy to sell myself and my services.

I was so happy with the changes I had experienced that I shared this technology with friends and family. My sister thought that subliminals were nonsense, but she had had a sleep problem for three years and so agreed to try the InnerTalk *Sleep Soundly* program. Within a short period, she was sleeping well again. I have a friend in sales, and I got him the InnerTalk program, *Powerful Selling and Closing*. My friend is now so happy because he is getting more cash deals than he has ever had. Things have improved so much for him that not only can he now retain sales recruits but they even come to him without his having to look for them.

I have now ordered a large number of programs and can always tell when I have "hit the nail on the head" because the results happen really fast. I still buy from Progressive Awareness on a regular basis because I am still exploring "how high is up," to use a term the sales representative introduced me to.

Name withheld, New Mexico

I have been using the CDs since I attended Eldon Taylor's lecture in December 2005. I am a therapist working with autistic and other special-needs persons, and I recommend that my clients use selected CDs based on their child's needs.

Since I have been listening to them myself, I realize that I am more accepting of others in my family, I feel less stressed, and I am able to cope well even in the midst of my hectic schedule. My business has also increased since I am open to the universe around me daily. I am beginning to go back to my early years in that I am able to find the time to appreciate my surroundings and the people in them.

In regards to my clients, I notice through my careful selecting of CDs for them based on their individual needs, my students are maturing in their own way, mentally and physically. They are more focused in their work, and attention spans have increased. Some of the parents have bought CDs for themselves and their other children.

The best thing about these CDs is that they are extremely relaxing. My stress level has been reduced tremendously and also the stress on the parents who have special needs children. They are feeling happy to be with their special needs child, and this helps the behavior modification work to proceed without much stress.

At the moment I am personally using eight CDs, and this is an investment for my life. The quality of my life has improved, especially with my husband. I am able to accept my challenges when I am challenged by my husband within our family life. In August we went to New Zealand for skiing. I attended ski classes at the resort, and I realized that I could not have been prepared for the mental and physical agility needed to endure the ski instructions. If I had done it before 2005, I would have collapsed with a lot of mental and physical stress and definitely lots of arguments with my husband in regards to skiing. Consistently using the CDs daily, even when I was in New Zealand, kept me very focused and concentrated during my ski classes. I choose my CDs every two months based on my needs as a therapist. We can participate in any program or training for our personal needs, but the key to it is to be **consistent** with the choice of training that we have undertaken for our life. So for me personally I would continue to reach out to others to use the CDs for friends and relatives and also for persons with special needs.

Thank you, Eldon Taylor.

Mary Anne Joseph Bekking, Malaysia
B. Phil. in Education (specializing in autism)
Therapist for Special Needs Persons
www.myautisticmalaysia.com

I just wanted to give you some feedback relative to your "Quantum Younging" work. I know we volunteered to be part of the program, but I just haven't had a chance to have photographs done, and then I completely forgot about it. I am really sorry. On a positive note, I have a few customers who have subscribed directly to your newsletter, and in February and March I got together with them, and the main issue of discussion was the physical changes I have experienced using the InnerTalk programs. I was even bold enough to bring out the wedding photographs and show them. We made some notes, and even I was amazed at the physical changes I have experienced, and thought I would share my discoveries with you.

I have been using the *Ultra Success Power* and *Ending Self Destructive Patterns* CDs extensively in the last 18 months and the results for me have been wonderful.

1. I have had gray hair since I was 27—I am now 34, and I haven't had any gray hair for 12 months.

2. My weight has always been erratic, bouncing between 48 and 58 kgs (105.6 and 127.6 pounds) which makes me about 5 to 10 kg's underweight. I have maintained my weight at 62 kg's for 12 months.

3. I had an accident which left scarring down the right side of my face when I was 17, and the scar color has noticeably faded for the last 12 months, so much so that the marks are barely noticeable.

4. I have no wrinkles left on my face at all.

5. This is the most measurable improvement: my bra size has increased by two sizes.

6. I used to suffer from migraines and was taking about 8 painkillers a day. I haven't had a migraine for more than 12 months. That might not be a physical change, but the migraines were a result of eye strain due to the intensity of the graphic work I did. I can focus for much longer periods of time now.

I am definitely healthier, stronger, and much more relaxed. Just wanted to let you have some feedback on my physical improvements and experiences with the products.

Mands, S. Africa

Amanda has all along been very independent with her schoolwork as long as a timetable was given to her. However, lately she has slackened a little. Before things got worse, I decided to give a try to the *Accelerated Learning and Study* CD that my colleague told me about.

After ten days of Amanda's listening, I certainly observed changes in her behavior. She is less obstinate. During the teaching session with her, she is less argumentative and is more willing to accept comments or constructive feedback that I give her. Another great change with her is that Amanda always lacked the initiative to practice her piano, but now she will tell me "Mum, I have not practiced my piano," and the next thing she will do is practice her piano after finishing her homework!

As for Andy, he is more confident and cries less. Last Tuesday, I was taking my rest at home. I observed Andy automatically do his homework. After that he switched on the computer and accessed MSN, which he has **never** done before! Shortly afterward, he went to play the piano! I thought I saw Amanda and not him. My hubby was shocked too. Andy actually remembered and followed what Amanda has been doing. He was learning to log onto the computer for MSN and playing the piano on his own.

Isn't this great! Confidence, powerful memory, self-motivation to learn, do one thing at a time, etc. The Innertalk CDs work; it delivers what it promises! We love our two kids very much. We are certain that they are now on the right track about **learning** and will be **enjoying** each and every day of their **learning journey**."

Felicianna Tay, Singapore

I purchased *Positive Mental Attitude* about one year after I went through a relationship breakup. I could not get myself together. I knew full well that my negative attitude would eventually slay me—but I couldn't stop. A friend found your Website and urged me to give it a try. That was almost 6 years ago. Within a few weeks of listening, I felt like it wasn't hard to breathe or smile. I started to feel like me again—until I looked in the mirror. After a year of sobbing, I had let myself go. My skin was nasty, my hair was a mess, and I smoked too much. So I purchased *Forever Young, Fit and Healthy* and listened to it faithfully. Two months later my uncle visited from Florida. He took one look at me and said, "I have my beautiful niece back. Thank God you look healthy again."

Then it came time to ditch the cigarettes. I was smoking at least 30 a day (maybe more). I got the program, and the funniest thing was, I brushed my teeth more, always trying to get the nasty taste out of my mouth. After 8 days I was down to 11 cigarettes, and then I spooked. I really did not want to let them go, so I stopped listening. I stayed with my 11 a day for years after, but I never enjoyed them. They had become a burden. So I dug out the program again, and within 6 weeks it was over. I understand they are almost $8 per pack now!

I have since recommended your programs to some people and purchased some myself for those who I really believed would benefit from them but might not really go all the way to purchase them. One friend became a better bowler. A family member became pregnant after years of fertility issues.

One more thing—*Power Imaging*—hopefully we can get more of them in the future? I purchased the *Optimal Weight Loss* and lost 10 pounds. When I put it on, it was so soothing I did not want it to end. Thank you, Eldon Taylor, for your brilliance. And thank you, Ravinder, for your patience and kindness.

Name withheld, New York

This has largely been the story of my journey or personal growth. It might be said that much of it is self-serving and that's fair enough, I guess, but equally true is the fact that each of us can genuinely only speak to each other from our own experience.

The stories of all of the people in this book are themselves examples of how each of us can empower ourselves if we only but choose to believe in the unlimited power within. The common denominator with every story is a simple truth: believing in yourself does matter!

It is this author's hope that by sharing just a few of the stories that have been sent to me and by telling my own, that you the reader will gain some insight into the how, what, why and so forth of self-imposed limitations and at least a couple of solid exit strategies for leaving those limitations in the past, if not for yourself, then for someone you care about.

A Word of Caution

It is a common tactic of naysayers, especially those with any so-called academic clout, to dismiss ideas of merit by using a tactic easily described this way: "One good belly laugh is worth a thousand syllogisms." This approach seeks to discredit not only through "the subtraction game" but also through immense ridicule. It may take courage to ignore this tactic if it comes your way, but that too is perfectly within your power. You will never know what you might imagine if you never think the question: *What would I do if I knew I could not fail?* You will never achieve a goal if you cannot imagine it. You will never break out of self-imposed or "chicken" learned limitations if a little criticism or ridicule dissuades you. Again, I repeat because it cannot be overstated, *Within you is the power!*

*** ***

*Character cannot be developed in ease
and quiet. Only through experience of
trial and suffering can the soul be strengthened,
ambition inspired, and success achieved.*
— Helen Keller

CHAPTER THIRTEEN

In Conclusion

There are a few slogans, words from the wise, that I try to remain in touch with. Robert Schuler said, "Better to do something imperfectly than to do nothing flawlessly." The words of Jerome: "Begin to be now what you will be hereafter." And finally, Napoleon Hill states: "Both poverty and riches are the offspring of thought."

It is written that each of us is a gift from God, and all that we become is our way of returning that gift. I am reminded of a line from a scene in the inspirational fiction work by Angelina Heart, *The Teaching of Little Crow*. In the scene the hero of the story has a moment of enlightenment as a result of understanding that "every blessed and loving thing you freely put out to the world, whether it be thought, feeling, words, deeds, or money, returns with more of its kind." He pauses and declares, "No wonder Jesus Christ instructed us to love our enemies. What we send out must come back to the creator, magnified."

The movie *The Celestine Prophecy* has a beautiful scene that is visually portrayed even better than in the book, in my opinion. In this scene, the ninth insight shows itself as a result of those receiving energy sending it back to the sender. The energy grows exponentially in this exchange. If you think of this energy as the unconditional love energy that begins with Creation and animates all, then it is easy to see how sending it back would increase it.

Dr. Joe Rubino, in his book *Restore Your Magnificence*, reminds us that the origins of self-doubt are often the result of misinterpretations of self or limited awareness. In his words:

"Misinterpretations damage self-esteem and run your life. Freedom comes from reinterpreting your past with compassion for your humanity and that of others."

This has been a book sharing both a little bit of myself and what I have learned, interpreted, and reinterpreted many times. I was born into a religious family. I worked hard, attended church every Sunday, studied, and reread what I had studied. At a very young age I was ordained in the priesthood, but many things didn't quite square with logic, reason, or consistency of the doctrine. I continued seminary studies but asked hard questions. I remembered what I was supposed to remember so I could take exams and get A's. However, when it came to term grades, I was admittedly shocked to find I'd flunked. Well, I was not abashed, so I took the matter up with the academic authorities and during review was informed that the grade would be changed to an A provided I never came back. It seems I had become a disturbing force in the classroom.

I took my A and left seminary. I became quite bitter and agnostic, if not atheistic. For many years I enjoyed beating up the so-called theological scholars. I lost myself completely. I forgot the miracles in my life and focused on the inadequacies of organized religion, the club that demanded your dues. Then came my awakening, not all at once, but slowly, over time. Fortunately, the Universe was patient. I found myself writing philosophical proofs for a Divine Creator and rereading all the sacred literature. In my small book *Exclusively Fabricated Illusions,* I finally set forth the problem that in my view disappoints so many people. The exclusive role of authority, "I have the only right way, and if you fail to follow it, you'll ____!" (You get the picture.)

In the sacred documents of all living religions is a fountain of truth. It can be said this way: "Whatever you do unto the least of them, you have done unto yourself." Martin Luther King once stated, "We must live together as brothers or perish together as fools." In that inter-related whole exist all of us. We may have been taught differently in our own little chicken yards, but the fact is simple: We are all one.

**"Whatever you do unto the least of them,
you have done unto yourself."**

I hope this work has shed some light on how and why we might find ourselves limiting our own realizations and beliefs and therefore reality. The mind is an absolutely awesome power, and we still don't know its potential. We do know that it modulates the body in many ways and can be our best friend or our own worst enemy. I would encourage you to take whatever you have gleaned from this book and continue in your progress to becoming all that you might be. I would suggest that you begin with reflection, questioning any and all thoughts that limit your potential good for self and society. I do strongly urge you to follow the good-deed theme presented earlier, together with the other suggestions for improving the quality of your life.

I also want to urge you to begin meditating. Meditation is a powerful tool; it is, after all, getting quiet and listening to the still small voice within. "Be still and know." It's easy to meditate and quite natural as well. Begin by choosing some simple word and repeat it with each exhalation. Just close your eyes, relax back, let go, and clear your mind by repeating something like "peace" with every exhalation. Soon the mind stills and a new vista of feeling and thought manifests. Many classes, tapes or CDs, and so forth can be of great assistance when it comes to acquiring inner peace and inner knowing. Use them if they are available to you, but with or without them, seek that inner noetic sense of your real being, life's true meaning and value—in short, seek the "peace that passeth understanding," for within this space your higher-self emerges.

So, in conclusion, we have convoluted the model. Our purpose is service, not taking. Our warm fuzzy feeling provides peace, balance, harmony, and improved health. Our recognition of the good in all works like a magnet to attract the right people and things into our lives, including our most endearing and loving relationships. Our prosperity is assured, for in the moment we always have everything we need, and ironically, we keep getting more when we stop trying to just make money. We bring our best with joy to whatever our task may be and that is not only recognized but rewarded. We are not pitiful creatures here to suffer but rather gifts from our Creator endowed with true co-creative powers. Our belief propels our lives with optimism and integrity, not a pack full of bad-luck fortune-cookies. We give to give, not out of some codependent bargain based on what we get back or control of some kind over another. We forgive and release blame; no more "get even and evener." We take responsibility and improve every day in every way.

One of the material findings from my work and the InnerTalk technology that is worth mentioning is how it works. First, a little digression. When exit polls are performed following many motivational events, the vast majority of attendees report a positive result and pledge to incorporate their new tools and learnings into their lives upon returning home. However, when we follow up with these people a month later, we learn that indeed most have not applied what they learned. There are always reasons (excuses) for this failure. Some may say something like, "Well, I thought about it, and it's just not right for my personality." Others claim that they simply have not had the time. Some say they tried, but it just didn't work. For the most part, it's all excuses. The fact is, just as I have suggested, if your inner mind (subconscious) does not believe it, you won't do it. Remember the "million dollar" characterization and Mr. Bill Gates? No amount of flashing lights, brilliant mirrors, loud music, and rah-rah alone can persuade the subconscious to let go of its adaptations and mechanisms. In other words, if you stand in front of the mirror and say to yourself, meaningfully and deliberately, statements that the subconscious disagrees with, it is only a matter of time before the inner talk (self-talk) within begins to undermine those statements. Then in some automatic servo loop way, the old behaviors just reassert themselves and that's the end, at least for the moment, of the desired change.

With the InnerTalk technology, all we need to do is listen, and we can do that as background while we watch television or even sleep. One hour a day for thirty days, and somehow something just magically seems to change. The change can seem dramatic and often happens even faster than expected, as you saw in the last chapter in the comments sent to me by users of InnerTalk. The reason for this seeming magic, and it's not magic at all, is that the subliminal beliefs in the subconscious mind have been massaged sufficiently to allow the stream of consciousness or self-talk to reflect the affirmations contained on the InnerTalk program, and voilà, change is easy.

For the record, I have often been asked why we have more than 400 titles. "Are we attempting to create perfect people?" I believe you and everyone else is already perfect, albeit many may be asleep or have not fully awakened to their divine potential. No, the reason we have as many titles as we do is to meet everyone where they are. Indeed, one of the original driving forces behind title development came from prison systems. Inmates wanted bodybuilding, weight lifting, and so forth. Fine, I reasoned, and we'll include the forgiveness set and esteem/responsibility elements in all. We did. In other words, the essential elements to taking responsibility, forgiving, appreciating, and otherwise beginning the process of awakening is on every single program we make, regardless of title. In fact, let me share a personal story with you as it may shed additional light on my personal perspective.

A few years ago I was asked to speak at a prestigious gathering of hypnotherapists, hypnotists, and psychotherapists. Every year for several years I had spoken at this event, so of course I accepted. The night before I arrived was the typical welcoming banquet for all participants. After the meal an older woman, who was a staff member of the school sponsoring the event and seated at the head table, lit a cigarette. A man in the audience promptly stood, walked to her table, jerked the cigarette from the woman's hand, scolded her loudly while suffocating the cigarette in her ashtray, and returned to his seat wagging his finger at her all the way. She broke into tears and ran from the hall.

To protect this gentle lady's anonymity, I'll just call her Penny. She was a lovely lady who went the extra mile helping students at the school, and many in the audience were either students or graduates. She was well known by all, and in my book, she is a wonderful woman with a golden heart who loved helping others.

I was told of this event before speaking, and I changed my entire presentation there and then. I began with, "I want you all to imagine that the word is out, the news has traveled around the world, and all know that the best of the best in health-care professionals are gathered here today to share and sharpen their skills. The professionals at this august gathering are noted as the best because their interest is genuinely in helping others. They are sensitive, caring professionals, and they know the power of their words can create wellness as well as dis-ease. They are all aware that the oldest woman on the planet lived well into her hundreds and died only when her doctors told her to stop smoking or die.

"Because this meeting was of such very high caliber, three special people were on their way to attend the gathering. Let's just imagine these three people, say, Buddha, Edgar Cayce, and, if you will, even Jesus. Now, our Buddha is the Buddha of Indian origin, not the Buddha of Chinese history, who is often portrayed as thin. So our Buddha is plump. Cayce, the well-known mystic healer who made literally thousands of readings while in a trance, healing as many people, is a chain smoker. Jesus' well-known statement, paraphrased, says it all: "It's not what you put in your mouth but what comes out of it, that will be your undoing."

Now, I continued, "So here are our three visitors. They have influenced and healed the lives of more than anyone can count, and here is what is going to happen. One third of you will run to Buddha and tell him you can help him lose weight. One third will run to Cayce and inform him that you can help him stop smoking and by the way, you'll tell them both that if they do not do something about it, it will kill them. The remaining third will no doubt offer to assist in keeping Jesus kosher, for everyone knows the story wherein Jesus is caught eating the wrong bread on the Sabbath and he was, after all, a rabbi.

I went on following this introduction to point out how wrong it was for Penny to have been humiliated and treated in such an undignified manner the night before. I pointed out that judging people and even possibly suggesting sickness on them in this way was irresponsible. I received quite nice applause but was never invited back to speak.

The bottom line for me is not about the usual concerns regarding body image and so forth. No, as a matter of fact (and as I have shown in my book *Wellness: Just a State of Mind*), one is much more likely to experience dis-ease as a result of a psychological predisposition, including how we handle stress, etc., than from enjoying chocolate. For me, it's all about waking up and claiming your true divine potential. Sometimes this happens one small step at a time, like the longest journey of Lao-tzu. One success, whether it's winning at basketball or losing weight can lead to building more confidence and empowering individuals to believe in themselves. That's why at InnerTalk the motto is, "When believing in yourself matters." This builds quality of life, and quality of life is, after all, what we all ultimately define as a successful life.

InnerTalk . . . When believing in yourself matters.™

Now, whether or not you ever use an InnerTalk program, I challenge you to take positive steps as soon as you put this book down. It might be easy for you to just sort of wait until tomorrow to begin to practice the simple fundamentals suggested here. Tomorrow never comes. Begin right now to take steps to actively practice forgiving and forgetting. Begin now to seek out opportunities to do at least two good turns every day. Take paper or buy a diary and begin to write down those little "helps" that you give to others. Write down your feelings. When you go to bed each evening, think about the day and record your good deeds. Take those thoughts to bed with you. I promise that you'll be surprised at what happens to your sleep, dreams, health, and happiness.

You may even discover memory landmarks that bring back warm, fuzzy feelings. I experienced one recently with a big smile on my face, and my wife asked what the smile was for. I told her of a clerk who had gone out of his way to help me, despite my error. You see, the last time I had seen him was months before. On that day he was down. His body language, facial expression, and general demeanor spoke for him. When I stepped up to the counter, I simply said, "Joe, what are you doing? You look younger!" At first he looked puzzled.

"No, I'm serious, Joe. You look like you've taken ten years off." (Joe is approximately sixty.) "Even your complexion looks younger and healthier. What are you doing?" I continued.

Joe said, "You really think so, Doc?"

"Yes, Joe. I mean, look at yourself, you're even standing straighter, and that smile on your face must be telling your brain to turn up all those good neurochemicals," I responded as I watched Joe follow the suggestion and stand straighter with a smile.

"Well, Doc, you've made my day," he said. "You need to come back more often," he added with a rich smile and gleam in his eyes.

My lovely wife added, "So this is another of your 'fake it till you make it' strategies, and Joe made it."

Indeed, that's where we all begin. We make the choice to smile, engage the world with joy and awe, do our good turns, and otherwise share the love with which we fill our hearts to overflowing. In the beginning, we may need to fake it. Sooner or later, though, the brain actually does turn on positive healthy neurochemicals as a mechanical reaction to smiling, our faking takes hold and we become what we pretend to be.

I know you get the picture, so please begin to act now. Life is a miracle and living a joy! You are a miracle and a gift, and you repay the gift by being all that you were created to be. Soar, my Eagle Friend.

*** ***

Acknowledgments

I am indebted, as usual, to my lovely wife for both her encouragement and her perseverance in assisting the editing process. Thank you, Ravinder. I would also like to thank Suzanne Brady for her extensive editing and re-editing.

Over the years, especially during times of controversy, there have been special people who have served almost as my living angels. To them—especially Roy, Lois, and Pat—words cannot adequately express my appreciation.

I am also indebted to the many who have gone before me and whom I cite as inspiring and leading me in my own development.

I also acknowledge the thousands who have written me to offer their thanks for my work that has made a difference in their lives. I cannot express in words just how meaningful these notes and letters are to me.

It is also important that I acknowledge a wonderful lady who shared a truly life-shaping experience with me—thank you, Connie.

Finally, thank you, each of you, for reading this work.

*** ***

APPENDIX A

Science of InnerTalk®

InnerTalk is based on more than 18 years of research and development. It is the only such technology to have been repeatedly independently researched and demonstrated effective by researchers around the world. Although this technology was patented under the name *Whole Brain,* it is now more commonly referred to as InnerTalk. Here is a brief overview of a few of the studies that have demonstrated the effectiveness of this technology:

1985–1986—In a double-blind study at the Utah State Prison, which was performed by McCusker, Liston, and Taylor, the Whole Brain technology was deemed effective in altering *self-esteem* among inmates. As a result, the Utah State Prison installed and maintains a voluntary tape library for inmates.

1988–1990   Cosmetic surgeon R. Youngblood and surgical staff tested the effect of the Whole Brain *Pre and Post Operative* tape on 360 patients. They reported a decrease in anesthetic requirements of 32 percent by volume as compared to a historical control group.

1990—In a double-blind study carried out at Colorado State University, it was found that using the Whole Brain program *Freedom from Depression* for more than 17 hours led to a significant decrease on the Beck Depression scale. This study not only shows the effectiveness of the Whole Brain program but also indicated that the effectiveness of the programs was dosage related.

1990—A double-blind study was carried out at Weber State University on the effects of the Whole Brain program, *Freedom from Stress.* The psychological test results showed a significant decrease in stress.

1991—A double-blind study conducted by Prof. Peter Kruse at Bremen University in Germany, using a specially created Whole Brain program, strongly demonstrated the influence of the program on decision-making. Kruse said, "The Taylor Method works!"

1991—Experimental psychologist Dr. Julian Isaacs investigated the effects of the following Whole Brain programs: *No More Procrastination, Time Management, Confidence Power, Freedom from Stress, Positive Relationships, I Am Assertive,* and *High Self-Esteem.* After three studies, it was concluded that the programs produced significant positive results that were verifiable.

1988–1991—The findings from a longitudinal study on the Whole Brain program for cancer showed that 43 percent of the patients who used the program went into remission. For the other patients, who eventually passed away, the average life span beyond the original prognosis was significantly extended.

1991—A study carried out by Professor R. B. Pelka of Munich University in Germany on a Whole Brain tape for weight loss showed average weight losses of 13 pounds in subjects who used the program without following any other kind of diet or exercise regimen.

1993—Diana Ashley at the University of Southern California studied the effect of Whole Brain on academic achievement in a double-blind experiment. Her conclusion found a significant increase in learning among students in the experimental group.

1993—Kim Roche of Phoenix University studied the effect of Whole Brain with children diagnosed as having Attention Deficit Hyperactive Disorder (ADHD) in a double-blind experiment. Her findings indicated a significant positive effect.

1993—Thomas Plante, faculty member of Stanford University and director of Mental Health Services for the Children's Health Council, together with Michael DiGregorio, Gerdenio Manuel, and Bao-Tran

T. Doan of Santa Clara University, evaluated the effect of Whole Brain on test anxiety in a double-blind experiment. The statistical data significantly supported the hypothesis that Whole Brain subliminal technology could be an effective tool in lowering test anxiety.

1997—Under the direction of Maurice P. Shuman, Jr., general director of Special Programs of Instruction, a pilot study was conducted by Duval County Public School System at the Pre-Trial Detention Center in Jacksonville, Florida. Twenty-two incarcerated juveniles participated in a study program using InnerTalk programs designed to assist in preparation for GED examination. The GED final test results show that 18 of the 22 troubled students passed the full GED examination.

1998—Combining InnerTalk *Weight Loss* audio and video with Echo-Tech audio and a special nutritional program developed and marketed by Oxyfresh International, Dr. Harbans Sraon, a biochemical geneticist of the University of California at Irvine conducted a 90-day weight-loss study. Dr. Sraon coached each subject to visualize their clear goal in terms of body fitness and reviewed progress weekly. Sraon reported that 90 percent of the subjects (10 men and 15 women) lost significant amounts of weight.

1998—Under the direction of Dr. Jose Salvador Hernandez Gonzalez and on behalf of the Institute of Mexicano Social Services (Medicas), 25 patients were exposed to both video and audio *Freedom from Dental Anxiety* tapes for 30 minutes prior to treatment and 30 minutes during treatment. The conclusion was as follows: "The use of InnerTalk before an integral odontologic treatment is 100 percent effective, reducing patient's anxiety and the noise made by the high speed hand piece used in this type of work, and furthermore, reducing the pain suffered by comparison to previous experience." The report goes on to recommend InnerTalk: "Therefore it is convenient to promote, among dental surgeons, the use of InnerTalk to improve their patients' comfort and achieve a better collaboration to treatments."

2002 (September)—Jane Alexander, independent journalist and researcher in the United Kingdom, ran her own study on the efficacy of InnerTalk. Independent testers worked with *Ultra Success Power, Neat and Tidy, Attracting the Right Love Relationship,* and *Jealousy.* All of the testers reported positive results.

2002 (November)—Jane Alexander, independent journalist and researcher in the United Kingdom, investigated several alternative methods for weight loss. Not only did she find significant weight loss using the CD for weight loss, but she did a price comparison between the different alternative treatments. Her cost comparison on a per pound of weight loss basis, showed costs of £26/lb for acupuncture (approx. $41.60), £11.42/lb for hypnotherapy (approx. $18.27), £29.28/lb for homeopathy (approx. $46.85), and £3.28/lb for InnerTalk (approx. $5.25).

2003—The results of a UK trial on the InnerTalk program titled *Breast Enlargement* was published in *What Medicine,* summer 2003 issue. "This trial involved 15 women and resulted in approximately 2cm of breast growth and a fuller cup size within 30 days. Women also reported a 'tingling sensation,' similar to that experienced in puberty."

Numerous clinical studies with single and multiple subjects have also found effectiveness with Whole Brain in areas as diverse as anorexia and dyslexia. Additionally, Whole Brain has been credited by professional coaches for significantly contributing to winning sports events ranging from football championships to national and Olympic judo medals.

*** ***

APPENDIX B

Abstract of Findings
by Charles F. McCusker, Ph.D.

Thirty-eight male residents (average age, 23) from the unit at the Utah State Prison completed the Thurstone Temperament Schedule in a voluntary participatory study. Following administration, subjects were randomly placed in one of three groups (experimental, 14; placebo, 13; and control, 11). The experimental group received and played a subliminal tape for 20 days. The placebo group received and played a similar sounding tape without an embedded subliminal message, while the control group had no tape exposure. At the end of 20 days a second Thurstone Temperament Schedule was administered. In the experimental group, 5 subjects remained who had completed the procedure, 3 in the placebo group and 8 in the control group. Others were lost due to discharges or unwillingness to participate.

In a comparison of the experimental and control groups, the following results were obtained. The Dominance scale scores decreased while the Reflective and Stability scale scores increased in the Experimental group (desired effects). The Dominance scale scored increased while the Reflective scale scores decreased in the Control group. These are interesting results across groups. In the experimental group, these results would be predicted by focus of the embedded subliminal messages. In the placebo group, the opposite effect obtained may be explained by the fact that they (the subjects) listened to a tape without a message and felt no change. They obtained no reinforcement to continue and possibly experienced some frustration.

It is emphasized that this pilot study had limitations, especially in terms of implementation and sample size.

It is not the intention of the experimenters to generalize beyond the obtained results. It must be emphasized, however, that to evaluate an incarcerated population was a unique opportunity; to our knowledge this was the first time subliminal technology has been evaluated with this population. The results indicated change and strongly suggest the need for further research with benefit to these individuals and society in general, as this technology is better understood and applied in a wide variety of applications and settings.

Experimental			Control		
Predifferences to postdifferences			Predifferences to postdifferences		
Scale Movement	Variable	Rate of Change	Scale Movement	Variable	Rate of Change
↑	Stability	+3.4	↑	Stability	+8
↑	Reflectivity	+2.6	↓	Reflectivity	-1.0
↓	Dominance	-2.7	↑	Dominance	+1.4

Endnotes

1. Kirshnamurti, J. 1991. *The Collected Works of J. Krishnamurti, 1948–1949: Choiceless Awareness.* Dubuque, Iowa: Kendall/Hunt Publishing Company.

2. Libet, B., Alberts, W. W., and Wright, E. W. 1976. "Responses of Human Somatosensory Cortex to Stimuli Below Threshold for Conscious Sensation." *Science*, 158 (3808), 1597–1600.

3. Joseph, R., ed. 2002. *NeuroTheology: Brain, Science, Spirituality, Religious Experience.* San Jose, Calif.: University Press.

4. Bach, Richard. 1976. *Jonathan Livingston Seagull: A Story.* New York: Avon.

5. Phillips, David. 1994. "Does Belief Influence the Outcome of Certain Diseases?" *The Lancet*, 342: 1142–45.

6. Langer, Ellen J. 1990. *Mindfulness.* New York: Perseus Books Group.

7. Locke, S., and Colligan, D. 1986. *The New Medicine of Mind and Body.* New York: E. P. Dutton.

8. Andersen, S. M., and Chen, S. 2002. "The Relational Self: An Interpersonal Social-Cognitive Theory." *Psychological Review*, 109, no. 4, 619–45.

9. Kierkegaard, S. 2002. Edited by H. Hong and E. Hong. *The Essential Kierkegaard.* Princeton, N.J.: Princeton University Press.

10. Korzybski, Alfred. 1994. *Science and Sanity: An Introduction to Non-Aristotelian Systems and General Semantics.* 5th ed. Englewood, N.J.: Institute of General Semantics.

11. McTaggart, Lynne. 2002. *The Field: The Quest for the Secret Force of the Universe.* New York: Harper Collins.

12. Taylor, Eldon. 1988. *Subliminal Learning: An Eclectic Approach.* Medical Lake, Wash.: R. K. Books.

13. Boston University. 2005. "Boston University Psychologists Find Neurological Mechanism for Subliminal Learning." **www.brightsurf.com.**

14. Mill, John Stewart. 1961. *Essential Works of J.S.M.: Utilitarianism, Autobiography, On Liberty, The Utility of Religion.* Edited by Max Lerner. New York: Bantam Books.

15. Jampolsky, Gerald. 2004. *Love Is Letting Go of Fear.* Berkeley, Calif.: Celestial Arts.

16. Taylor, Eldon. 1990. *Subliminal Communication: Emperor's Clothes of Panacea.* 2nd ed. Medical Lake, Wash.: R. K. Books.

17. Taylor, Eldon. 1995. *Thinking Without Thinking: Who's in Control of Your Mind?* Medical Lake, Wash.: R. K. Books.

18.   Epley, Nicholas. 1999. "What Every Skeptic Should Know about Subliminal Persuasion." *Skeptical Inquirer*. Sept–Oct.

19.   Bornstein, R., and Masling, J. M. 1988. *Empirical Perspectives on the Psychoanalytic Unconscious*. Washington, D.C.: American Psychological Association.

20.   Ellis, Albert. 1988. *How to Stubbornly Refuse to Make Yourself Miserable about Anything—Yes, Anything*. New York: Lyle Stuart.

21.   Wolman, B. B. 1973. *Handbook of General Psychology*. Englewood Cliffs, N.J.: Prentice-Hall.

22.   Bower, Bruce. 1993. "Neandertal Neck Bone Sparks Cross Talk - Hyoid Fossil May Indicate Capacity for Speech." *Science News*. page 262.

23.   Hauser, Marc, and Andersson, Karin. 1994. "Experiments and Observation on Vocal Communication and Acoustic Perception in Captive Cotton-top Tamarins and Vervet Monkeys." *Science News* May 21, page 333.

24.   Rossi, Ernest. 1993. *Psychobiology of Mind Body Healing: New Concepts of Therapeutic Healing*. New York: W. W. Norton and Company.

25.   Fosar, Grazyna and Bludorf, Franz. 2003. *Vernetzte Intelligenz*. Aachen: Omega-Verlag

26.   McTaggart, Lynne. 2002. *The Field: The Quest for the Secret Force of the Universe*. New York: Harper Collins.

27.   Lipkin, Richard. 1994. "Simulated Creatures Evolve and Learn." *Science News*. 146. July 23, page 63.

28.   Laszlo, Ervin. 1994. "Genius Hypothesis." *Journal of Scientific Exploration*. 8, no. 2, 257–67.

29.   Weiss, Peter 1999 "On the Origin of Circuits." *Science News*. 156, Sept. 4, page 156.

30.   Sheldrake, Rupert. 1995. *The Presence of the Past: Morphic Resonance and the Habits of Nature*. Rochester, Vt.: Park Street Press.

31.   Hagelin, J. S.; Rainforth, M. V.; Orme-Johnson, D. W.; Cavanaugh, K. L.; Alexander, C.; N. Shatkin; S. F., Davies; J. L., Hughes; A. O.; Ross, E. 1999. "Effects of Group Practice of the Transcendental Meditation Program on Preventing Violent Crime in Washington, DC: Results of the National Demonstration Project June–July 1993." *Social Indicators Research*, 47, 2, 153–201.

32. Schwartz, Gary. 2002. *The Afterlife Experiments: Breakthrough Scientific Evidence of Life After Death.* New York: Pocket Books.

33. McTaggart, Lynne 2007. *The Intention Experiment.* London: Harper Element.

34. Krishnamurti, J. 1987. *The Awakening of Intelligence.* San Francisco, Calif.: Harper & Row.

35. Laing, Robert. 1976. *Politics of Experience.* New York: Ballentine Books.

36. Joseph, R., ed. 2002. *NeuroTheology: Brain, Science, Spirituality, Religious Experience.* San Jose, Calif.: University Press.

37. Foundation for Inner Peace. 1996. *The Course in Miracles.* New York: Viking.

*** ***

Recommended Resources

Arntz, William. Dir. 2005., *What the Bleep Do We Know!?* Twentieth Century Fox Home Entertainment.

Bach, Richard. 1976. *Jonathan Livingston Seagull: A Story.* New York: Avon.

Cousins, Norman. 1991. *Anatomy of an Illness as Percieved by the Patient.* New York: Bantam.

Beattie, Melody. 1986. *Codependent No More: How to Stop Controlling Others and Start Caring for Yourself.* Center City, Minn.: Hazelden.

Boone, J. Allen. 1939. *Letters to Strongheart.* Upper Saddle River, N.J.: Prentice Hall.

Capra, Fritjof. 1997. *The Web of Life: A New Scientific Understanding of Living Systems.* New York: Anchor.

Dyer, Wayne. 2006. *Inspiration.* Carlsbad, Calif.: Hay House.

———. 2005. *The Power of Intention.* Carlsbad, Calif.: Hay House.

Foundation for Inner Peace. 1996. *A Course in Miracles.* New York: Viking.

Gill, Mel. 2000. *Uncommon Sense.* Singapore: Pandora Publishing.

King, Godfré Ray. 1934–2003. *The "I Am" Discourses.* Schaumburg, Ill.: Saint Germain Press.

Goswami, Amit. 2001. *Physics of the Soul: The Quantum Book of Living, Dying, Reincarnation, and Immortality.* Charlottesville, Va: Hampton Roads.

Guillory, William. 1987. *It's All an Illusion.* Salt Lake City, Utah: Innovations International.

———. 1985. *Realizations.* Salt Lake City, Utah: Innovations International.

Harper, Charles L., Jr., ed. 2005. *Spiritual Information: 100 Perspectives on Science and Religion.* West Conshohocken, Penn.: Templeton Foundation Press.

Hawking, Stephen W. 1988. *A Brief History of Time: From the Big Bang to Black Holes.* New York: Bantam.

———. 2001. *The Universe in a Nutshell.* New York: Bantam.

Heart, Angelina. 2005. *The Teaching of Little Crow.* Virgin, Utah: Heart Flame Publishing.

Houston, Jean. 1997. *The Possible Human: A Course in Enhancing Your Physical, Mental and Creative Abilities.* New York: Tarcher/Putnam.

James, William. 2005. *The Compounding of Consciousness.* Whitefish, Mont.: Kessinger Publishing.

——. 1992. *The Correspondence of William James, Vol. 1–3.* Charlottesville, Va.: University Press of Virginia.

——. 1978. *Essays in Philosophy.* Cambridge, Mass.: Harvard University Press.

Jampolsky, Gerald. 1988. *Love Is Letting Go of Fear.* Berkeley, Calif.: Celestial Arts.

——. 1984. *Teach Only Love.* New York: Bantam.

Keyes, Ken, Jr.. 1984. *The Hundredth Monkey.* Camarillo, Calif.: DeVorss.

Key, Wilson Bryan. 1976. *Media Sexploitation.* New York: Signet.

——. 1980. *The Clam-Plate Orgy.* New York: Signet.

Krishnamurti, J. 2004. *Beginnings of Learning.* New York: London: Phoenix.

——. 1987. *The Awakening of Intelligence.* New York,: Harper & Row.

——. 1991. *The Collected Works of J. Krishnamurti, 1948–1949: Choiceless Awareness.* Dubuque, Iowa: Kendall/Hunt Publishing Company.

——. 1987. *Krishnamurti to Himself: His Last Journal.* New York: Harper & Row.

——. 1972. *You Are the World.* New York: Harper & Row.

——. 1963. *Life Ahead.* New York: Harper & Row.

Laing, R. D. 1965. *The Divided Self.* New York: Pelican Books.

——. 1976. *The Facts of Life.* New York: Pantheon Books.

——. 1976. *The Politics of Experience.* New York: Ballantine Books.

Langer, Ellen J. 1990. *Mindfulness.* New York: Perseus Books Group.

Lewis, C. S. 1961. *The Screwtape Letters.* New York: Macmillan.

Lipton, Bruce. 2005. *Biology of Belief: Unleashing the Power of Consciousness, Matter, and Miracles.* Santa Rosa, Calif.: Elite Books.

Marie, Terri. 2005. *Be the Hero of Your Own Game: A Guide to Master the Game of Life.* Ontario, Canada: Tiki Books.

Maslow, Abraham H. 1993. *The Farther Reaches of Human Nature.* New York: Penguin.

McTaggart, Lynne. 2002. *The Field: The Quest for the Secret Force of the Universe.* New York: HarperCollins.

——. 2007. *The Intention Experiment.* London: Harper Element.

Mill, John Stuart. 1975. *On Liberty.* New York: Penguin Books.

Oates, David. 1991. *Reverse Speech: Hidden Messages in Human Communication.*

Indianapolis, Ind.: Knowledge Systems, Inc.

Packard, Vance. 1984. *The Hidden Persuaders*. New York: Pocket Books.

Rossi, Ernest. 1993. *The Psychobiology of Mind-Body Healing: New Concepts of Therapeutic Hypnosis*. New York: W. W. Norton & Company.

Rubino, Joe. 2003. *Restore Your Magnificence: A Life-Changing Guide to Reclaiming Your Self-Esteem*. Boxford, Mass., Vision Works Publishing.

Schwartz, Gary. 2002. *The Afterlife Experiments: Breakthrough Scientific Evidence of Life After Death*. New York: Pocket Books.

Singer, Peter Albert David. 2001. *Writings on an Ethical Life*. New York: HarperCollins.

Springer, S. P., and Deutsch, G. 1998. *Left Brain, Right Brain*. New York: W.H. Freeman and Co.

Talbot, Michael. 1992. *The Holographic Universe*. New York: HarperPerennial.

Taylor, Eldon. 1992. *Wellness: Just a State of Mind?* Medical Lake, Wash.: R. K. Books.

———. 1987. *Little Black Book*. Medical Lake, Wash.: R. K. Books.

Twain, Mark. 2004. *Letters from the Earth: Uncensored Writings*. Reprint. New York: HarperPerennial Modern.

Watts, Alan W. 1975. *Psychotherapy East & West*. New York: Vintage.

———. 1966. *The Book: On the Taboo Against Knowing Who You Are*. New York: Pantheon Books.

Wittgenstein, Ludwig. 1973. *Philosophical Investigations: Remarks on the Philosophy of Science*. 3rd ed. Upper Saddle River, N.J.: Prentice Hall.

Yogananda, Paramahansa. 1979. *Autobiography of a Yogi*. Los Angeles, Calif.: Self-Realization Fellowship.

*** ***

About the Author

Eldon Taylor has made a lifelong study of the human mind and has earned doctoral degrees in psychology and metaphysics. He is a Fellow with the American Psychotherapy Association (APA) and a nondenominational minister.

Eldon was a practicing criminalist for over ten years while completing his education. He supervised and conducted investigations and testing to detect deception. His earliest work with changing inner beliefs was conducted from this setting, including a double-blind study conducted at the Utah State Prison from 1986 to 1987. Eldon is president and director of Progressive Awareness Research, Inc. For more than 20 years, his books, tapes, lectures, and radio and television appearances have approached personal empowerment from the cornerstone perspective of forgiveness, gratitude, and respect for all life. Eldon now lives in the countryside of Washington State with his wife and their two sons. Apart from his family and work, his true passion is horses.

***

Visit Our Website

If you enjoyed this book and would like to learn more about the tools suggested to help you become the person you were meant to be, visit our website at **www.choicesandillusions.com**.

*** ***

InnerTalk Distribution

U.S.A.
Progressive Awareness Research, Inc.
PO Box 1139
Medical Lake, WA 99022
1 800 964 3551
1 509 244 6362
www.innertalk.com

U.K.
Vitalia Health
The Marina, Harleyford Estate
Henley Road, Marlow, Bucks Sl7 2DX
UK
011 44 1628 898 366
www.innertalk.co.uk

Germany
Axent Verlag
Steinerne Furt 78
86167 Augsburg
Germany
011 49 821 70 5011
www.axent-verlag.de

Mexico
Dialogo Interno
Calle Retorno Cerro De Acazulco No. 6
Col. Oxtopulco Universidad Del. Coyoacan
Mexico D.F. C.P.04318
Mexico
011 52 555 339 5742
www.dialogointerno.com.mx

**Malaysia/Singapore/Brunei/Australia/
New Zealand/Papau New Guinea**
Progressive Awareness Sdn Bhd
2-2 Jalan Pju 8/5E, Perdana Bus. Cntr.
Bandar Damansara Perdana,
47820 Petaling Jaya
Selangor, Malaysia
011 60 37 729 4745
www.innertalk-au.com
www.innertalk.co.nz
www.innertalk.com.my

Taiwan and China
Easy MindOpen
3F, No. 257, Ho-Ping East Rd. Sec. 2
Taipei, Taiwan, R.O.C
011 886 (227) 010-468(1)
www.iamone.com.tw

Distribution Inquiries

For information regarding distributing
InnerTalk programs, please contact:

Progressive Awareness Research, Inc.
PO Box 1139
Medical Lake, WA 99022
1 800 964 3551
1 509 244 6362
www.innertalk.com

Hay House Titles of Related Interest

EVERYDAY WISDOM FOR SUCCESS, by Dr. Wayne W. Dyer

THE LAWS OF THINKING: 20 Secrets to Using the Divine Power of Your Mind to Manifest Prosperity, by Bishop E. Bernard Jordan

POWER OF THE SOUL: Inside Wisdom for an Outside World, by John Holland

REPOTTING: 10 Steps for Redesigning Your Life, by Diana Holman and Ginger Pape

SAYING YES TO CHANGE: Essential Wisdom for Your Journey, by Joan Z. Borysenko, Ph.D., and Gordon F. Dveirin, Ed.D. (book-with-CD)

SOUL LESSONS AND SOUL PURPOSE: A Channeled Guide to Why You Are Here, by Sonia Choquette

THE TIMES OF OUR LIVES: Extraordinary True Stories of Synchronicity, Destiny, Meaning, and Purpose, by Louise L. Hay & Friends

WHAT TO DO WHEN YOU DON'T KNOW WHAT TO DO, by Wyatt Webb

YOUR DESTINY SWITCH: Master Your Key Emotions, and Attract the Life of Your Dreams! by Peggy McColl

***

All of the above are available at your local bookstore,
or may be ordered by contacting Hay House (see next page).

***